Words Brushed by Music

JOHNS HOPKINS : POETRY AND FICTION
John T. Irwin, General Editor

Twenty-Five Years of the
Johns Hopkins Poetry Series

Words
Brushed by
Music

Edited by JOHN T. IRWIN

WITH A FOREWORD BY ANTHONY HECHT

The Johns Hopkins University Press
Baltimore and London

This book has been brought to publication with the generous
assistance of the Albert Dowling Trust.

The Johns Hopkins University Press
2715 North Charles Street
Baltimore, Maryland 21218-4363
www.press.jhu.edu

Library of Congress Cataloging-in-Publication Data

Words brushed by music : twenty-five years of the Johns Hopkins
poetry series / edited by John T. Irwin
    p. cm. — (Johns Hopkins, poetry and fiction)
ISBN 0-8018-8028-9 (alk. paper) — ISBN 0-8018-8029-7 (pbk. : alk. paper)
1. American poetry—20th century.   I. Irwin, John T.   II. Series.
PS615.W648 2004
811′54080896073—dc22   2004009044

A catalog record for this book is available from the British Library.

Contents

Foreword

In these early days of the twenty-first century, an aspiring young poet who has assembled what looks like a solid book's worth of poems and has started to cast about for a possible publisher has in prospect what may seem like a rich multitude of options, but which in hard fact is not quite so ample. The young poet is likely to find that the major trade publishers, who already have under contract the big wheels in whose august company it would be ever so comforting to appear, have closed their lists and are unable to take any new and untried talent. I personally know of a case where such bottom-line considerations prevented a publisher from taking a very fine book by an unknown. At the other end of the spectrum there are those fly-by-night small presses, doubtless prepared to take a fling at anything but without the means to do much in the way of promotion or advertising. So money governs both ends of the field.

Happily, between them stands the admirable institution of the university press. While more modestly endowed than the trade publishers, university presses are more firmly based than the small ephemeral presses, and they have clear, identifiable character to their lists. Poetry published by, for example, the University of California Press can be identified a mile away as altogether different from the poetry on the lists of the University of Chicago, or Yale, or Princeton, or Wesleyan. Surveying all options, the poet will at least have to decide to which orthodoxy of style and subject matter his work belongs—there being no longer anything that can be called heterodox, even the most wildly "experimental" being now no more than another convention.

John T. Irwin, editor of this volume, has briefly attempted to characterize in his preface the work here assembled, and he has announced his "governing criteria" in both positive and negative terms. They are grounds that seem sound. But an abstract expression of principles carries far less weight than the eloquence of the poems Irwin has chosen. I have read through these with great care, with surprising pleasure, and, in not a few cases, with admiration and delight. And the best index I can give by way of registering my satisfaction is to say that I found a full sixty poems that seemed to me to range anywhere between delightful, deeply moving, and out-right superb. Who are the poets these writers themselves admire? I asked myself. And a mildly investigative reading produced at least four names: Frost perhaps first of all, then James Wright, Auden, and Samuel Beckett. These are all writers of stature and of seriousness. Which does not, of course, mean that all the poets here are serious in some lugubrious way. There's a good deal of fun to be found, for that matter, even in Beckett, and Frost, Wright, and Auden gave way to levity on occasion.

As Irwin indicates, the first poet published in this series was the well-established and greatly admired John Hollander, one of whose contributions, "Blue Wine," is a dazzling fantasia, departing from several premises: that since conventional wine is commonly either red or white, only blue is needed to compose the tricolor emblem of France; that Homer's sea is "wine-dark" and the fluid base of adventure, not alone for Greek heroes but for the great adventurers of eighteenth- and nineteenth-century novels, and thus the native element of the imagination. (Not for nothing is the poem dedicated to Saul Steinberg.) At one point in the poem a composite pilgrim/adventurer called "We," in a land unknown but clearly European in character, is greeted by a child who comes forth with an offering of the local wine. "It was blue," the poet tells us and, with fine Hollander irony, dismisses the entire Hollywood (tinseltown) enterprise by adding, "reality is so Californian." But "Blue Wine" is only one of Hollander's varied contributions, others being characteristically wry, Audenesque, and sotto voce.

I can't, of course, proceed to single out the merits of all the poets whose work I admire, but since I began with the work of a well-established male poet, let me commend now the work of a less well-known female poet, Adrien Stoutenburg. In a poem called "Mote," about a hummingbird (a daring, Dickinsonian topic, see "A Route of Evanescence"), she views the tiny creature in swiftly changing images, mimicking its speed:

> Here we have a minute thunder,
> mandolin, banjo, fever,
> potential crisis of motion
> as in a spinning jenny
> grown eccentric, its cotton raveling
> into a knot like a flower.

The poem beautifully concludes:

> But when he comes, shining the window,
> and leans there, gleams in his cape,
> tips his javelin and remains,
> we lay down our books, music, cards,
> and watch like the cats
> who are also our boarders,
> as helpless as they
> to stay that mote by talons or love.

Hollander and Stoutenburg are but two among a large selection of remarkably gifted poets, diverse in their styles and concerns but at one in their skillful determination to engage the reader, to practice their art with all the dexterity at their command, to give simple, outright pleasure. And what more could a reader ask?

The Johns Hopkins University Press has done itself proud in offering publication to these poets, so different from one another yet so akin in their striving for excellence. And with a policy of loyalty to its contracted authors, the Press hopes to keep the work of these poets alive and available to readers, now and in the future. What such a volume as this does for the reader is to offer a rich Swedish smorgasbord of appetizers, allowing the interested to browse and select, to relish and compare, and then, having found something that satisfies, to get hold of the poet's work from which the samples in this volume were selected.

Anthony Hecht

Preface

The Johns Hopkins Poetry and Fiction series began in 1979 as a joint venture between the Johns Hopkins University Press and the Johns Hopkins Writing Seminars. In 1977 when I returned to Hopkins as chair of the Writing Seminars after having edited *The Georgia Review* at the University of Georgia for three years, I suggested to Jack Goellner, then director of the Press, that since collections of poetry and short fiction had become endangered species in the publishing world, the Johns Hopkins University Press could provide a real service to the field of literature by sponsoring a series of such books. I further suggested that the Writing Seminars would seek extra funding to underwrite the project. With the help of then-Provost of the University Richard Longaker, we were able to dedicate income from two endowments—the G. Harry Pouder Fund and the Albert Dowling Trust—to support, respectively, the fiction and the poetry titles we published, and in March 1979 the series began with the appearance of John Hollander's *Blue Wine and Other Poems* and Guy Davenport's *DaVinci's Bicycle*.

In the years since, the series has published thirty-one volumes of poetry and forty volumes of fiction. The present volume, which culls the best poems we've published, and a second volume slated to appear in early 2005, which will collect the best short stories we've published, mark the series' twenty-fifth anniversary.

This project began with two simple guiding principles: to publish works of poetry and fiction exhibiting formal excellence and strong emotional appeal and to publish writers at all stages of their careers whether they be first-book authors, writers in mid-career, or authors summing up a life's work in a retrospective collection. We have also on rare occasions brought back into print volumes published elsewhere that we felt deserved a longer life in bookstores and the closer attention of readers. The governing criteria in selecting the poems for this volume, as in selecting the poetry collections for the series, were that the chosen works put to full use the musical component of the English language, that they be humanly moving (since if a poem doesn't move us, who cares what else it does?), and that they be about things of a certain substance and importance, things of interest to intelligent, cultured adults (no navel-gazing, no interior monologues meant not so much to be heard as overheard, exhibiting the self-congratulatory, narcissistic exquisiteness of the monologist's "sensibility," no ideological special-pleading overriding and demeaning the poem's status as an aesthetic object). What attracts one in a poem is not much different from what attracts one in a person—wit, elegance, wisdom born of experience, mastery of language. That said, the best illustration of what we looked for in the poetry selected for the series is represented by the poems that follow.

I would like to dedicate this twenty-fifth anniversary volume to all those at the Johns Hopkins University Press whose work and devotion have made this series possible, to the Johns Hopkins University administration and to my colleagues in the Writing Seminars who have supported it, and to all the poets whose work appears here and who have over the years made this series both successful and a pleasure to edit. Finally, I'd like to thank my research assistant Ms. Hillary Yablon for her help in preparing the manuscript of this volume.

Words Brushed by Music

JOHN BRICUTH

FROM   1981

The Heisenberg Variations

Song of the Darkness

For Zelda Fitzgerald

Beneath a striped umbrella
Whose brown sunlight is rain,
My colors melt and run.
There's an old ache in my brain.

Set your face in a smile—
Rough grains within a glass
Will char the fragile neck.
The sick never get well.

What was the tune I laughed?
Just once I knew myself
Falls before the leaf
Broke the sun in half.

Darling, why don't you come?
We could waltz, and whirling, you
Would forget words they say,
Loving the steps I do.

Strands of the musical stave,
Twisted with spikes of time,
Score the white throat.
My wires catch and sting.

Who said it was ill
To love by giving pain?
If time cures the sick,
The sick never get well.

Villanelle: "We're Dancing Now . . ."

We're here with all our friends we've known since college.
Our teeth are straight and our hair is mostly blond.
We're dancing now and you're missing it and it's great.

I've been practicing in my room all afternoon.
I've been trying to get the knack but I don't know.
These are the steps but they don't fit the music.

All the girls we brought are incredibly relaxed.
We understate and our eyes are mostly blue.
We're dancing now and you're missing it and it's great.

If this is amusing, I don't get the joke.
If this is a trick, I fail to see the humor.
If these are the steps, why don't they fit the music?

There's a girl here we'd really like for you to meet.
Her teeth are straight and her hair is mostly blond.
She's dancing now and you're missing it and it's great.

It's always like this. Why is it always like this?
Listen, we'd like to see you, but it's getting late.
If these are the steps, why don't they fix the music?
We're dancing now and you're missing it and it's great.

Talking Big

for Harry and Claudia

We are sitting here at dinner talking big.
I am between the two dullest men in the world
Across from the fattest woman I ever met.
We are talking big. Someone has just remarked
That energy equals the speed of light squared.
We nod, feeling that that is "pretty nearly correct."
I remark that the square on the hypotenuse can more
Than equal the squares on the two sides. The squares
On the two sides object. The hypotenuse over the way
Is gobbling the grits. We are talking big. The door
Opens suddenly revealing a vista that stretches
To infinity. Parenthetically, someone remarks
That a body always displaces its own weight.
I note at the end of the gallery stands a man
In a bowler and a black coat with an apple where
His head should be, with his back to me, and it is me.
I clear my throat and re (parenthetically) mark
That a body always falls of its own weight.
"whoosh-whoom!" sighs the hypotenuse across,
And (godknows) she means it with all her heart.

The Touch

for Mona Van Duyn

Having attended her first piano requital in which
Numerous old musical scores were settled,
Chopin run over and rolled into a ditch
When Bach's light velocipede hard-pedalled
Went wheeling by, its (grand piano-) forte speed,
I blink at the chromatic scale of humane endurance,
Tone-, stone-, or simply deaf and dull
And wink in the first Euterpean lull
At the girl fit to ride down every nuance.

Only a small matter of a small only daughter,
Save music, as a kind of Vinteuil's phrase expanded
Of the heart-divining rhythm that can't be trained,
By absence must leave her seldom keyed to the laughter
Nor quite secure though beautiful, high-handed,
As one to whom things must often be explained.

JOHN BURT

FROM   1996

Work without Hope

Love and Fame

She'd smiled as if she knew him. That kept him up
And scared him some, but more, excited him.
And in the dark, while his brother coughed next door,
He lay awake, wondering about that girl,
Who'd caught his eye just as she tossed her head
To laugh her shy delicious laugh—at what
He never learned—then handed him that smile
And vanished in the intermission crowd
While he just stood there thinking what to say.
That's what it's like. That's what it must be like.
(He hadn't seen it happening to him.)
They look back at you. That changed it all.
But would he ever see that girl again?
His brother coughed and choked. He lit the lamp
And brought a glass of port to still the spasm.
"Just stay a bit, John, won't you?"
                                 "Yes, of course.
I'm wakeful anyway."
                    "Still, I'm sorry."
He wiped the sweaty forehead with the sheet.
"Shh. Go back to sleep. I'll sit awhile."
Would he have the chance to love that girl,
Or any of the girls (or are there any?)
Who might look back at him in just that way?
It was her gift, a secret, like a poem
She might, just from the blue, have handed him
Clear and whole and wholly eloquent
And never to be written, like the rest.
At the window he could count them: one,
Then two, then three drops falling in the dark,
And to the dark, stars swept from the sky
Flashing downward silently all night.
Give me this hour, God, if nothing else.

What Ellen Said

She hadn't said it. What was it she said?

He leaned both hands there, on the sink, and watched
That pale thin face regard him stupidly:
An old man running water from the tap,
As if to fill the cup he wouldn't take.
It had not changed. That disappointed him:
Then nothing ever leaves a mark on me.

The boy, he knew, had drifted back to sleep
In what was still his room, unused awhile.
"She was glad you came," he'd tried to say.
"I'm not sure she saw me."
                        "Yes, she did.
I'm sure she did."
                  "We can't know that, Pop.
I didn't even see her move her lids."
They'd sat an hour. "Pop, let's go to sleep,"
He'd said at last, like talking to a child,
"There's nothing we can do now anyway."
"I'm O.K. You sleep. I won't be long."

The faucet spluttered. Across the hall she lay
As he had left her, in her little room.
That night, before he'd called the boy, he'd asked
Again and again, "Ellen, are you there?"
Her eyes were closed. He knew she was awake.
"Ellen, has it been worth it after all?"
He knew she was awake. She closed her eyes.
"I have to know."

"Oh, God," she said at last.
And that was it. Later her breathing changed.

He turned the water off. The house was cold.
And nothing happened. Nothing ever would.

1938

for David Murray

They had to haul it to the earth with ropes,
The gang of men who brought the airship in
Those last few feet just short of round the world
In record time. That noon they'd put up flags
And built a vantage for the newsreel men,
And the governor himself came to the pier
To watch them warp it down. Was it alive?
It humped itself, prow first, a little up,
And then the tail fins delicately kicked,
And turned a fraction over.
                              "Boys, pull again,
Just one more time. Before the wind comes up."
And each one had a thought.
                              "No, hold it down."
And back through chains of men the straining rope
Sang out like a bowstring shooting home,
And men locked arms around the waists in front.
"Together, boys.
                  For Christ's sake, one more time."
But it was over. First three or four let go,
And then the gang dissolved to save itself,
And who was left, the steadfast foolish, maybe
Or maybe just the paralyzed from fear,
Or maybe just the last to feel the shudder
As all at once the rest of them dropped off,
Some six or eight, were hoisted into air.
Most of these let go at twenty feet.
But two held on, and the airship, breaking free,
Shot straight up at the sun triumphantly
Beyond all holding on or holding out.

One man, spread-eagled, hit the hangar roof;
The other thrashed and churned down to the trees
As if to swim the air. But neither screamed.
No one watching them recalled a sound.

I do not know, had I been there that day,
That I'd have held—or if I should have held.
I couldn't pull that airship down alone.
But could we all? I don't know even that.
Could I have kept those men somehow in line?
And if I had, might that have killed us all?
I know those men woke nights, despised themselves,
Saw in their dreams those two come crashing down.
By now they, too, are dead; their moral flinch
Is past extenuation, and past blame.

THOMAS CARPER

FROM

Fiddle Lane

1991

Turning in Bed

The stench of early cruelty returns
As I, a child, crouch underneath low boughs
Playing with candles. In small pans the worms
Writhe. Now I grow, and from a neighbor's house
He runs at me, screaming that I have hid
His toy gun, which I get and, with a blow
That terrifies me, smash it to his head,
Causing blood and my blinding tears to flow.
The picture breaks. I ache. The sheets are taut.
I turn for comfort, then return to hell,
Fleeing across a fiery space and caught
By images assaulting me until
I fear I will not wake again, but keep
Revolving painfully on the spit of sleep.

That's a Nice Leg

She's nine and worries. That midsummer day
We who were guests had left the dining room
After breakfast, a few had gone to play
Tennis, and I was thinking of a swim.
Lisa had her suit on, and was standing
Next to me, so we talked. "You've been here often?"
"Just twice." "Will you be going to the landing?"
"When Mommy comes." Perhaps my voice did soften
When I said, "That's a nice lake," for she heard
"A nice leg," and with ages-old concern
Pressed hers, and declared it fat. My word,
"Lake," repeated, caused her eyes to turn
Downward—as though a blossom could be bent
On closing from its own embarrassment.

Talking with Charlot

He had been hurt. He'd called me to the fence
Early that morning, but I hadn't gone.
Perhaps donkeys have something of human sense;
The greeting unreturned left him alone.
At noon he stood, as usual, at his wall,
His head against it, keeping away the flies.
Three times I called, with no response at all,
Or movement. I began to realize
He was as desolate as I'd often been
When failing to make my affection clear,
And so I walked quite humbly up to him,
And spoke it slowly in his donkey ear.
I didn't know if he would understand.
Later, he came and took bread from my hand.

I Am Just the Same

I am just the same as when
Our days were a joy, and our paths through flowers.

THOMAS HARDY

A world in pieces with the loved one gone.
The garden failing and the house a chill.
The bedroom a despair to look upon,
With flowers dying at the window sill.
Pictures of the places where no more
Two can be two are desolate in their frames.
The faithless clock ticks as it ticked before
They met in love and vowed to join their names.
Gazing about, he feels the urgent force
Of recent wishes rise up when her name
Comes to his lips, as though that great divorce
Had never happened. "I am just the same,"
He wants to tell her, passionately; "I lack
Youth only—and the hope to have you back."

Roses

During the night of fever, as she lay
Between an exhausted wakefulness and sleep,
I sat beside her fearfully, in dismay
When her slow breathing would become so deep
It seemed that she might slip beyond recall.
Then I would touch her; then she would revive;
Then, when her eyelids opened and a small
Smile would greet me, hope would come alive.
With morning, the ordeal was over. Gone
Was every trace of illness. A soft rain
Had swept across the countryside at dawn,
So even our garden was made fresh again.
Then Janet went among our roses where
She and the roses shone in luminous air.

From Nature

Funny Face

His muscles tensed like clockwork when he heard
A big one say, "Now make your funny face."
Setting himself to please, without a word
He'd put his twisted puckerings in place.
Big ones would be delighted. They would clap,
Call him a little wonder, and then turn
To grown-up talk. He'd slide from Mother's lap,
Cross the broad porch, escaping their concern,
And go down to his sandbox in the yard
Where he could listen to them overhead
While making hills and holes. Once, having starred
Again, he winced when someone sternly said,
"Tom will do anything to get a laugh,"
In tones that sounded like an epitaph.

How Mother Is

The people at the Care Center are kind,
And, as we live long distances away,
They send brief notes and photos that remind
Us of her irreversible decay.
We're glad to see her face at eighty-one
Still young, though hands are frighteningly thin,
With every bluish vein, and joint, and bone
Visible through a glassy sheath of skin.
We're told her eyes stay focused when they meet
Another's eyes, and that she seems content;
When nurses help her up onto her feet
She "walks at all times with encouragement."
She starts no conversation, although while
Another speaks, she does not cease to smile.

PHILIP DACEY

FROM   1981
The Boy under the Bed

Mystery Baseball

No one knows the man who throws out the season's
    first ball.
    His face has never appeared in the newspapers,
        except in crowd scenes, blurred.
    Asked his name, he mumbles something
        about loneliness,
        about the beginnings of hard times.

Each team fields an extra, tenth man.
    This is the invisible player,
        assigned to no particular position.
    Runners edging off base feel a tap on their shoulders,
        turn, see no one.
    Or a batter, the count against him, will hear whispered
        in his ear vague, dark
        rumors of his wife, and go down.

Vendors move through the stands
    selling unmarked sacks,
    never disclosing their contents,
    never having been told.
    People buy, hoping.

Pitchers stay busy
    getting signs.
    They are everywhere.

One man rounds third base, pumping hard,
    and is never seen again.
    Teammates and relatives wait years at the plate,
        uneasy, fearful.

An outfielder goes for a ball on the warning track.
   He leaps into the air and keeps rising,
      beyond himself, past
      the limp flag.
   Days later he is discovered,
      descended, wandering dazed
      in centerfield.

Deep under second base lives an old man,
   bearded, said to be
   a hundred. All through the game,
   players pull at the bills of their caps,
   acknowledging him.

Sleeping Parents, Wakeful Children

When our parents were sleeping
We brought them gifts
It was a whispering time
The great bodies lain down
Upon the long bed
The deep sighs adrift
Through the upper rooms
It was a whispering time
When the gods slept
And we made gifts for them
With paints paper and tiny
Scissors safe for us
Masks and rings
Obscure magical things
In the halted hour
In the still afternoon
The anger asleep
And the jokes we didn't understand
The violent love
That carried our weather
All subsided to these
Two vulnerable ones
Their hands and mouths
Open like babes'
Their heads high
In the pillowy clouds
For all we knew dreaming us
Sneaking in
Lest they woke and discovered
Our love our fear
How we thrilled to appease

Praise and thank
Them in secret
My sister and I
Approaching the border
The edge of the platform
Where the gods murmured
So precise in our placement
Of these our constructions
Frivolous fair
The gift on the skirts
Of their lives for surprise
Then turning away
Lips and fingers a cross
When they opened their eyes
They would never know how
When or why
They would never know
Who we were

The Living Room

I love to photograph people's living rooms
. . . and mirrors.

ELSA DORFMAN

This is the place where it all happened,
    Though no one knows precisely what.
Once there was a family here, then there was not.
    The scattered papers and overturned glass tend
To confirm those who lived here left in a hurry:
    An open window leads some to suspect
A natural occurrence—a wind, a vortex—
    Wrapped them up and blew them away;
Other, more level-headed authorities
    Believe if there was a wind it was one
Inside them, a kind of family wind
    That harried the blood but left the trees
Thoroughly unmolested. According to that
    Theory they blew themselves out
Of each other's lives with centrifugal
    Motion and haven't stopped yet.
Though there were children, it is impossible
    To determine the exact number,
For the discovery of both a mature
    Fingerprint on a toy by that end table
And certain words and phrases in a hastily
    Penned and half-finished letter
Suggests that calendar-age was no guarantee
    Against the, say, youthfulness of any member.
Pictures of ancestors crowd one wall;
    Whoever lived here had a sense

Of history, though whether the consequence
    Of that was an abiding good cheer
Or deep despair is a question still
    In need of an answer. Thus it is the mirror
Over the mantelpiece that deserves most
    Careful attention. Stand before it
And you can see behind you the dark ghosts
    Of those whose absence is at issue, yet
Turn around to catch them in your own
    Two eyes and they are gone.
Perhaps they disappear inside you,
    Like divers for treasure, some lost jewel
The family staked its reputation on
    And that now you alone,
Without your knowledge, carry. Or perhaps
    The ghosts themselves are treasure,
What you must redeem from behind glass
    And, at all times, proudly, wear.
But all that is speculation. What is not,
    However, is the richness of this carpet
We stand on. One could get lost
    In its design and easily pretend
The whole masterpiece is Being's ground,
    Despite, or because of, one badly worn spot.

Bedtime Song

To sleep in the house of children,
In the house that children sleep in,
Is to sleep in the arms of children's
Dreams, that are dreaming the house,
And to dream you are the children
That are sleeping themselves into dream.

And to sleep in that house is to sleep
In the children, who are the house,
Who are the dark you sleep in
And the arms that hold you asleep,
And to dream in that dark is to house
The children, and you, for the night.

To sleep in a house that dreams
Children is to sleep well, to arm
Yourself for the night is to sleep
In the childish dark, and to dream
Of waking is to waken the child
Who is yourself, dreaming

Of sleep in the children's house.

TOM DISCH

FROM   1989
Yes, Let's

In Defense of Forest Lawn

In his poem "Tract" William Carlos Williams
recommends a style for funerals
much like the style he practiced
as a poet: a "rough plain hearse"
resembling a farm wagon, its driver
demoted to walk alongside holding the reins,
and the mourners riding after
with conspicuous inconvenience, open
"to the weather as to grief."

In horse-and-buggy days, perhaps,
such a scenario might have worked,
but nowadays much-weathered wood denotes
deluxe accommodations. A triumph
for Williams' esthetics, but the problem
remains: how to bury people simply
and tastefully, without on the one hand
holding up traffic unduly or on the other
treating the corpse like industrial waste.

Personally I think that Forest Lawn
has got just about the right combination
of hokum and expedience, gravitas and pizazz.
People are inclined to laugh at Forest Lawn,
having been instructed by Evelyn Waugh
that only the Sovereign Pontiff can *own*
the Pietà, that Europe has the copyright
on class, and that Americans had better stick
to . . . . What would he suggest: farm wagons?

But if Romans did well to copy Greek originals,
if museums needn't be embarrassed by their casts—
if, that is, form and not seignoralty
is our ideal, then why shouldn't Forest Lawn
heap as much of the enmarbled past
on the plates of our grief as, say,
Westminster Abbey or St. Paul's? Why shouldn't
the dead, God damn it, be allowed one Parthian
shot at greatness? Aren't wakes for feasting?

Suppose we did it in the minimalist way
Williams suggests, bankrupting florists
and stonecutters. Do you think the heirs
in their enhanced prosperity would endow
posterity with anything so grand or lush
as a properly got-up cemetery? Think again.
How, I wonder, did Waugh himself get planted?
Opulently, I'm sure. So, gentlemen, if you'll step
Over here, I'd like to show you our brochure.

Entropic Villanelle

Things break down in different ways.
   The odds say croupiers will win.
We can't, for that, omit their praise.

I have had heartburn several days,
   And it's ten years since I've been thin.
Things break down in different ways.

Green is the lea and smooth as baize
   Where witless sheep crop jessamine
(We can't, for that, omit their praise),

And meanwhile melanomas graze
   Upon the meadows of the skin.
(Things break down in different ways.)

Though apples spoil, and meat decays,
   And teeth erode like aspirin,
We can't, for that, omit their praise.

The odds still favor croupiers,
   But give the wheel another spin.
Things break down in different ways:
We can't, for that, omit their praise.

D.W. Richmond Gives Directions to the Architect of His Tomb

As for the scenes at my office
I have nothing but praise for your work,
Just the amount of detail is extraordinary
& where your picture has departed from fact
I think I can see the reasons for what you've done.
However, I have two secretaries
& you have shown only one. Also, as I have pointed out,
I take frequent trips to Chicago,
staying there weeks at a time—& where
on the wall of this tomb is there any indication of that?

I have enjoyed your representation of my wife.
You manage to capture just those qualities
that make people love her. But somehow you miss
what it is that sets my son Richard apart.
At least you could show him carrying books, & in a
    darker suit.
My daughters, however, are excellent—so true to life!
But you must, beneath the figures, write their names:
Margaret is the one teasing a cat; while this is Laura
on the telephone; & the little one, Amy,
is alone in her bedroom, watching teevee.

As for this scene, where you have shown me at my
    pleasures—
this has been your masterpiece.
I have never seen such realism. Unfortunately,
however, I cannot allow these to remain here.
But if they could be detached—is this possible?—without
damaging the wall, I would pay whatever it would cost,

above and beyond that which has been agreed to already,
if you would re-install them in an apartment here in town.
I will furnish you with the address,
if you can accept so unofficial a commission.

Dark Verses and Light

The Joycelin Shrager Poems

i am just a plain poet

i am just a plain poet
the way pete seeger
is just a plain singer

no frills about what i do
you don't need big-deal critics
to tell you what my poems mean

i know i'm not as good a
poet as many others
who aren't as famous as me
but that's because they can't
speak to the audience i can

speak to the audience of people
who may not be very bright
or in the top third of their class
but who still want to be good

to be understood and appreciated

those are my people
you can't expect them to like
a subtle poet like john ashbery
(who i have to confess doesn't make
a scrap of sense to me)

not everyone is going to dig
even anne waldman who is my own
personal candidate for the greatest

    modern american poet (my friend
rod mckuen agrees) anne is so
damn life-affirming which is great
if you've got the sort of life
you want to affirm
                   a lot of us
don't we've got to work at lousy jobs
we're stuck in ratty apartments
we tend to be unpopular
except with each other

as i say these are my people
& my press Moonchild Press
communicates with them directly
on their own level because i
am one of them a moonchild
moonsister flesh of their
flesh mind of their mind

they aren't all simple people
by any means they aren't all good
they only want to be good
but they do think about things
like the meaning of life
they can recognize the loveliness
of stars & flowers & animals in zoos
& the terrible sorrow too

some of them have learned to love
deeply
      tenderly
           & true

the smart people have always listened
to my people's songs but they've never
heard their poetry
           until me
until Joycelin Shrager!

something people don't realize

something people don't realize
is how tragic it is to be fat
believe me it's no joke though
you'd never know that from the way
people act/ i suffer from overweight
& of course i'd like to look like
faye dunaway or leslie caron
but even at my most thin
seven years ago i was no
miss america/ my mother's
the same as me loves to eat
can't keep away from the icebox
can't stop snacking becomes deeply
depressed on the second day of a diet
she's learned the only way to be even a
little happy is to give in to cravings
right away/ they say fat people have
more of a sense of humor than the
rest of you/ i guess they don't
know about our tears i guess
they haven't seen us look
ashamed going into the
special departments
set apart for fatties
i guess when you're
thin it doesn't
matter much
what fat people
must suffer

i who have gone through the whole gamut

i who have gone through the whole gamut
of experience the heights of artistic
success & the depths of grief loss
& humiliation have this to say to you
the way to be happy is to live totally
in the present moment to give yourself
up to the buttercups of spring
& the beautiful green lawns of a summer
afternoon when you've sneaked into a
cemetery to surrender yourself completely
to a doubledip icecream cone to relax
in a warm tub & float along
with rimsky-korsakov's scheherazade
or look into a baby's eyes & think
he's mine i made him inside
my own body i brought him to birth
with my own pain   for even pain
can be creative even the death
of a dearly loved spouse can be a source
of joy when you look out the window
& realize that everything in the universe
is mysteriously connected to everything
else including our dear ones gone to rest
including you donald tho i may never
understand why you left me suicide
is always so foolish but never mind
i'll always love you anyhow

minor poets are human too

minor poets are human too
& when we go out in the woods
& marvel at mushrooms & lie in the
sand & flip out for a great symphony
what we're feeling then is as
important to us as whatever
it was that wallace stevens felt when he
wrote all those poems that no one under
stands

     but what's even harder to under
stand about wallace stevens is how he
could be an insurance salesman
all those years he was a poet
at the same time   you'd think
he'd be too tired when he got home
from a day of canvassing

          my father tried
to sell insurance for a while after the
bankruptcy & didn't get anywhere
except he did sell a big policy to poor
donald which led to my founding
Moonchild Press in 1976

it was the same insurance company
that wallace stevens worked for way
back when   everything connects
mysteriously to everything else
in the world of the spirit

bowling has been the great spirit

bowling has been the great spirit
ual experience of my life
i never thot i'd be able to do
anything physical until my friends
bonnie and donna took me to the bowling
alley just four blocks from where i live
& taught me to bowl
how to run up real fast
to the foul line & let rip
without thinking of where
the ball would go exactly
but just imagining the SMASH!
it'll make when it hits
zen bowling donna calls it
& it works at least for people
like me who rely on intuition
i'm bowling over 100 now
almost every game & tho
that may not seem like a lot
to most bowlers to me
it's pure glory

when i am sick science fiction

when i am sick science fiction
is my passion the more escapist
the better   none of that new
wave stuff   (that's for when i'm well &
prepared to meet challenges)

but conan & elric & tolkien
& anne mccaffrey those are my deities
i journey with them into the 4th
dimension of my head where i caress
the silken tresses of my steed & hear
the twanging of a magic harp

                              so imagine
how delighted i was this year
when my favorite sf author

            Silverbob

(that's robert silverberg in case
you didn't know) produced his first
novel in far too long combining
the jewellike mind-boggling intellectual
excitement of his New Wave achievements
with that old-fashioned Sense of Wonder
fans can go for   it's called

            lord valentine's castle
(any connection silverbob with
lord weary's castle by robert lowell
have i given away any secrets you sly fox)

well what can i say it was wonderful
his best book ever & it sold to paperback
for a lot of money too i'm told

so please silverbob please please
please keep writing don't
take another long vacation
like the last one when you thot
fandom hadn't been grateful we are
& to prove it i'm going to come
to the next worldcon & totally
smother you with appreciation
& silverbob remember
if you ever turn to poetry—
think of Moonchild Press

EMILY GROSHOLZ

FROM   1992
Eden

On Spadina Avenue

Driven by love and curiosity,
I entered the painted shops along Toronto's
Chinatown, and lingered
in one red pharmacy, where every label
was printed in mysterious characters.
Beside myself, not knowing what I stopped for,
I read the scrolling dragons, roots, and flowers
intelligible as nature,
and quizzed the apothecary on her products.

Lovesick for my husband. She was puzzled,
for how could I explain
my private fevers to a perfect stranger?
I questioned her obliquely, hit-or-miss:
Lady, what's this button full of powder?
What's this ointment in the scaly tube?
Who are these dry creatures in the basket
and how are they applied?
The deer tails gleamed in fat, uneven rows,
unrolled sea horses darkened on the shelves,
and other customers with clearer motives
stepped in behind my back.

I couldn't say, his troublesome male beauty
assails me sometimes, watching him at night
next to the closet door
half-dressed, or naked on the bed beside me.
An evening amorousness keeps me awake
for hours brooding, even after love:
how fast in time we are,

how possibly my love could quit this world
and pull down half of heaven when he goes.

The patient Chinese lady has no cure,
and serves her other customers in order.
Across the curled-up, quiet, ochre lizards,
giant starfish, quince, and ginger root,
she turns to look at me.
We both know I'm not ill with this or that,
but suffer from a permanent condition,
a murmur of the heart, the heart itself
calling me out of dreams
to verify my warm, recurrent husband
who turns and takes me in his arms again
and sleepily resumes his half of heaven.

Life of a Salesman

Behind the small, fixed windows of the album,
my father sits on sand, flowered with sea-salt,
nestling my younger brothers on his knees,
my mother beside him, me on another towel.

Or else he's smiling, lapped by shallow combers,
holding the kids so only their toes get wet,
free from booze and taxes, the city office,
his territory, miles of empty highway.

My husband, late addition to the family,
points out a disproportion: that generic
photo of my father on the beaches
stands for a man with two weeks' paid vacation.

I say to my brothers, look, you're all contented!
Both of you blue with cold in your ratty towels,
thrilled with the wind, the escalating waves,
our father watching the ocean roll its sevens.

Most of the time, he's on the road again
selling fancy letterhead, engravings
the businessmen he calls on can't be certain
they need, without his powers of persuasion.

He tries to tell them. Fifty weeks a year,
in sun and rain and snow, on secondary
arteries crosshatching the back country
of Pennsylvania, Maryland, West Virginia.

Alone at night in one more shabby diner,
his pale self in the speckled mirror-panels
is like a stranger's. He coats his potatoes
and minute-steak in catsup, for the color.

He wants a drink, but holds off for another
day, another hour. The gray Atlantic
shuffles invisibly. He orders coffee
and maybe calls his sponsor up, long distance.

Or calls my mother next, with lonely questions
she tries to answer, putting on my brothers
who sneeze and whistle, practice words like "daddy"
that touch him at the end of the connection.

The dial tone doesn't sound at all like waves.
He might go to a movie, or a meeting:
there's always one around to fill the shady
dangerous intervals of middle evening.

He likes the coffee's warmth, the sound of voices
circling in on wisdom: know the difference.
Protect him, higher power, when he travels
his hundred miles tomorrow, rain or shine.

His death lies elsewhere, hidden in the future,
far from his wife and children, far away
from cleanly riffled Jersey shores in summer,
the gray Atlantic playing out its hand.

Eden

In lurid cartoon colors, the big baby
dinosaur steps backwards under the shadow
of an approaching tyrannosaurus rex.
"His mommy going to fix it," you remark,
serenely anxious, hoping for the best.

After the big explosion, after the lights
go down inside the house and up the street,
we rush outdoors to find a squirrel stopped
in straws of half-gnawed cable. I explain,
trying to fit the facts, "The squirrel is dead."

No, you explain it otherwise to me.
"He's sleeping. And his mommy going to come."
Later, when the squirrel has been removed,
"His mommy fix him," you insist, insisting
on the right to know what you believe.

The world is truly full of fabulous
great and curious small inhabitants,
and you're the freshly minted, unashamed
Adam in this garden. You preside,
appreciate, and judge our proper names.

Like God, I brought you here.
Like God, I seem to be omnipotent,
mostly helpful, sometimes angry as hell.
I fix whatever minor faults arise
with bandaids, batteries, masking tape, and pills.

But I am powerless, as you must know,
to chase the serpent sliding in the grass,
or the tall angel with the flaming sword
who scares you when he rises suddenly
behind the gates of sunset.

VICKI HEARNE

FROM 1994
The Parts of Light

Riding Skills

They say you never forget
So you had sure better not
But you do. The light chuckles

To hear this, chuckles out loud
As you pick up your courage
With the reins. That's what happens

When you pick up the reins, legs
Better remember! because
Riding is remembering

To ask politely. The horse
May tell you her stable name,
Then the one she dances by,

Or may not, but if she does
The light stops its mocking,
Gets going on the smooth streets

Of the world. The horse's scope,
The confident cathedrals,
Allow truth its say as if

Riding were remembering.

The Dog and the Word

The catechism of dogs
is to attack
at a word, laugh

at another, so
it has been written
so consider

the flash of a Golden
Retriever, mouth so swift
on the pheasant, prairie

chicken, stick or ball, bit
of twine, so
tender, this divine

seizure that wants nothing more
for itself, stands
to deliver and reveals

in the bird dog's celebrant
profile the sky
to the naked eye. Grab

without greed, we
have no noun
for it, only

the one command.

Danes and Wolfhounds

Dignity: (rare but not obsolete) a
Great Dane, an Irish Wolfhound, a curve
of neck and thigh, graciousness
bowing to our disgrace,
the Dane survives

calumny and is the pride
of the *gebrauchshundesrassen*, the
noble group.

The Wolfhound's humor, no
malice only rosiness
as of a comfortable heart,

can take down wolves, which is how we know
wolves are the enemy.
                                                    Giants
Of forebearance, they think
with their chests and their thinking rides
the cathedral scope of their limbs. They breathe

in and breathe back the air
to nourish us. This is their gift,
a talent possessed

by other dogs, mastered
by these friends
of any landscape.

JOHN HOLLANDER

FROM   1979

Blue Wine and Other Poems

Blue Wine

for Saul Steinberg

1   The winemaker worries over his casks, as the dark juice
Inside them broods on its own sleep, its ferment of dreaming
Which will turn out to have been a slow waking after all,
All that time. This would be true of the red wine or the white;
But a look inside these barrels of the azure would show
Nothing. They would be as if filled with what the sky looks like.

2   Three wise old wine people were called in once to consider
The blueness of the wine. One said: "It is 'actually' not
Blue; it is a profound red in the cask, but reads as blue
In the only kind of light that we have to see it by."
Another said: "The taste is irrelevant—whatever
Its unique blend of aromas, bouquets, vinosities
And so forth, the color would make it quite undrinkable."
A third said nothing: he was lost in a blue study while
His eyes drank deeply and his wisdom shuddered, that the wine
Of generality could be so strong and so heady.

3   There are those who will maintain that all this is a matter
Of water—hopeful water, joyful water got into
Cool bottles at the right instant of light, the organized
Reflective blue of its body remembered once the sky
Was gone, an answer outlasting its forgotten question.
Or: that the water, colorless at first, collapsed in glass
Into a blue swoon from which it never need awaken;
Or: that the water colored in a blush of consciousness
(Not shame) when it first found that it could see out of itself
On all sides roundly, save through the dark moon of cork above
Or through the bottom over which it made its mild surmise

There are those who maintain this, they who remain happier
With transformations than with immensities like blue wine.

4 He pushed back his chair and squinted through the sunlight across
   At the shadowy, distant hills; crickets sang in the sun;
   His mind sang quietly to itself in the breeze, until
   He returned to his cool task of translating the newly
   Discovered fragments of Plutarch's lost essay "On Blue Wine."
   Then the heavy leaves of the rhododendrons scratched against
   Gray shingles outside, not for admittance, but in order
   To echo his pen sighing over filled, quickening leaves.

5 "For External Use Only?" Nothing says exactly that,
   But there are possibilities—a new kind of bluing
   That does not whiten, but intensifies the color of,
   All that it washes. Or used in a puzzle-game: "Is blue
   Wine derived from red or white? emerging from blood-colored
   Dungeons into high freedom? or shivering in the silk
   Robe it wrapped about itself because of a pale yellow chill?"
   One drink of course would put an end to all such questioning.

6 ". . . and when he passed it over to me in the dim firelight,
   I could tell from the feel of the bottle what it was: the
   Marqués de Tontada's own, *El Corazón azul.* I had
   Been given it once in my life before, long ago, and
   I tell you, Dan, I will never forget the moment when
   It became clear, before those embers, that the famous blue
   Color of the stuff could come to mean so little, could change
   The contingent hue of its significance: the truer
   To its blue the wine remained, the less it seemed to matter.
   I think, Dan, that was what we had been made to learn that night."

7 This happened once: Our master, weary of our quarreling,
    Laughed at the barrel, then motioned toward us for drink; and
    Lo, out of the sullen wooden spigot came the blue wine!

8 And all that long morning the fair wind that had carried them
    From isle to isle—past the gnashing rocks to leeward and around
    The dark vortex that had been known to display in its whorls
    Parts not of ships nor men but of what it could never have
    Swallowed down from above—the fair wind blew them closer to
    The last island of all, upon the westernmost side of
    Which high cliffs led up to a great place of shining columns
    That reddened in the sunset when clouds gathered there.
      They sailed
    Neither toward this nor toward the eastern cape, darkened by low
    Rocks marching out from the land in raging battle with the
    Water; they sailed around a point extending toward them, through
    A narrow bay, and landed at a very ancient place.
    Here widely-scattered low trees were watching them from the hills
    In huge casks half-buried there lay aging the wine of the
    Island and, weary half to madness, they paused there to drink.
    This was the spot where, ages before even their time, Bhel
    Blazed out in all his various radiances, before
    The jealousy of Kel led to his being smashed, as all
    The old tales tell, and to the hiding and the parceling
    Out of all the pieces of Bhel's shining. Brightness of flame,
    Of blinding bleakness, of flavescent gold, of deepening
    Blush-color, of the shining black of obsidian that
    Is all of surface, all a memory of unified
    Light—all these were seeded far about. There only remained
    The constant fraction, which, even after every sky
    Had been drenched in its color, never wandered from this spot.
    And thus it was: they poured the slow wine out unmingled with

Water and saw, startled, sloshing up against the insides
Of their gold cups, sparkling, almost salty, the sea-bright wine . . .

9   It would soon be sundown and a shawl of purple shadow
Fell over the muttering shoulders of the old land, fair
Hills and foul dales alike, singing of noon grass or Spanish
Matters. The wooden farmhouses grew grayer and the one
We finally stopped at, darker than the others, opened its
Shutters and the light inside poured over the patio.
Voices and chairs clattered: we were welcomed and the youngest
Child came forth holding with both hands a jug of the local wine.
It was blue: reality is so Californian.

10 Under the Old Law it was seldom permitted to drink
Blue wine, and then only on the Eight Firmamental
Days; and we who no longer kept commandments of that sort
Still liked to remember that for so long it mattered so
Much that they were kept. And thus the domestic reticence
In my family about breaking it out too often:
We waited for when there was an embargo on the red,
Say, or when the white had failed because of undue rain.
Then Father would come up from the cellar with an abashed
Smile, in itself a kind of label for the dark bottle.
At four years old I hid my gaze one night when it was poured.

11 Perhaps this is all some kind of figure—the thing contained
For the container—and it is these green bottles themselves,
Resembling ordinary ones, that are remarkable
In that their shapes create the new wines—*Das Rheinblau, Château
La Tour d'Eau, Romanée Cerulée*, even the funny old
Half-forgotten *Vin Albastru*. And the common inks of
Day and night that we color the water with a drop of
Or use for parodies of the famous labels: these as

Well become part of the figuring by which one has put
Blue wine in bold bottles and lined them up against the light
There in a window. When some unexpected visitor
Drops in and sees these bottles of blue wine, and does not ask
At the time what they mean, he may take some drops home
     with him
In the clear cup of his own eye, to see what he will see.

The Cable-Car

The cable-car is the easy way up
The great mountain we see from everywhere
And whose shadow falls outside the city.

The cable-car is the easy way up,
And as it swings on above dark ravines
I catch the first sight of her distant home.

The cable-car is the easy way up,
And thus I am breathless here at the top
Not from climbing, but at how far I see.

How high it is here, and how far I see!
From her window she cannot see how near
Her house is to the highway into town.

How high it is here, and how far I see!
The world we both move in is its own map:
From here, my house looks very near to hers.

How far it is here to the ground again!
I shall descend with joy, as if rising.
The cable-car is the long, slow way down.

The Patch of Garden

Two round, lovely hills stand above
The long descent of fair meadow
Down to where the small garden lies.
Shall we be there, as if once more
In the true place we were before?

The dry angel of day has turned
Away for a moment: leave him
To guard ruined temples among
The stony fields and the dead hills.

Quickly now, he is not looking:
Let us enter your own garden
Through the gateway in the soft hedge.
We shall be there, as if once more
In the true place we were before.

Piano Interlude

The air is emptied of song in this gentleness;
Our bed is by the window, and our own silence
Is like a curtain drawn back, allowing moonlight
To come harping through the window-blinds. Silver strings
Quiver on the ceiling, and here your heartbeat half-
Enters my ear; my text is your skin on my tongue;
Below us our limbs are composed in a tender
And intricate figure not to be read aloud.
Song is not born in rooms emptied by fulfillment,
But only in long, cold halls, hollow with desire.

Special Sessions

Imprisoned in this court of law,
I hear the guarded lawyers drone
On in a halting monotone
And may not even read or draw,

But, the sole juror of my case,
Sequestered in my present fate,
Wearily I deliberate
The future's bleak and silent face.

Though turnkey Time may set me free
From dark courts of the loins and heart,
I shall not ever have "the part
Of Justice, which is Equity".

Waiting is virtue, act is crime
In life where justice is reversed:
For me the sentence has come first,
The verdict will emerge in time.

From a House Party

Here in this splendid, silly room—
Mullions and oaken linenfold—
The past aped by the rather old—
My ear in pain, my heart in gloom,

Beneath the faint sneer of Augustus
(Above me stands his marble head)
I read that Audrey G. is dead,
Likewise, the bearded J.R. Justice.

I sorrow in this pine-green air.
Back where you are, garbage and thugs
Abound, the cats tear up the rugs,
The summer's shadows grow. Somewhere

A dropped glass smashes on the floor;
The household-gods are breaking up.
Soon there will be one last cracked cup
And I shall love you all the more

As now, so much more than I could
Then, when we bound ourselves to—what?
—Unbrokenness we thought our lot,
Children of the enchanted wood.

JOSEPHINE JACOBSEN

FROM   1995

In the Crevice of Time

Suite for All Clowns' Day

CLOWNS' MARCH

Ladies! And likewise Gentlemen!
We are the clowns, we are the Clowns.
We were baptized with the mot juste—
Joey, and Charlie, and Auguste;
Our names are more than names—are nouns.
We are the clowns, your several Clowns.

Under the lights, and in the dark,
We are the clowns, we are the Clowns,
And we have learned that dogs do bark
Not only at beggars in the dark.
Our fingers gloved, our faces doughy,
Our titles Charlie, and Auguste, and Joey,
We are the clowns, your several Clowns.

Parade before you, cleansed of caution,
We are the clowns, we are the Clowns,
Alike your nightmare and your potion,
We are your trinity sans caution
Your loss and victory sans parley.
We, Joey, and Auguste, and Charlie,
In your small hearts, in your tall towns,
We are the clowns, your several Clowns!

CLOWNS' TURNS

I
Charlie never had any dignity, Charlie didn't.
His intention was starry but his luck was foul;
He tried very hard to save his soul,

But if dividend and divisor fetch the quotient,
Charlie was hopeless. His agape was strong,
But his inventory wasn't worth a song.
And Charlie never had any dignity, Charlie didn't.

Charlie tried to be brave, wanted to be clever,
He knew a lot and was on the right side,
But something uproarious happened to his pride,
He never triumphed, never, never, NEVER.
You could call him a hero fairly or a boob,
A citizen of the city of God or a terrible rube,
Certainly he wanted to be brave and tried to be clever.

Charlie wept tears, but Charlie was a comic.
He pickled the sick, the inept, the old, in brine,
But prat-falls and custards were in Charlie's line,
His gifts were funny rather than histrionic—
He tried for dignity, but dignity slipped him,
He tried for magnitude, but his big shoes tripped him.
Charlie wept tears, but Charlie was a comic.

II

As I swing from his tail the hooves of the galloping roan
    batter before my nose,
Then I must let go and roll in the sawdust shame and away
    he goes.
But a gleaming general told me, Joe, I haven't a man that
    brave.
The ringmaster willing, I could walk his tight-rope till
    doomsday's duck and after,
But I cheat my spine and the balls of my feet and I flail and
    I fall in the laughter.
But a judge in his robes said, Joey, you know more about
    rope than J. Ketch or a sailor.

In the brittle winter's waste with sweat and pride I shape
    my difficult game
And hotly I wait for the flowering spring, to pluck my
    public shame.
But a scarecrow saint in the ripe corn said, Brother, I am
    His patient clown.

III
Caesar and saint of court and canvas,
August Auguste, you come to try
The children crowded under canvas
You never meant to terrify.
Too thickly lashed the little eye.
The giant mouth is red. Mechanic,
Juggler, dog-walker, laugh or cry,
The undercurrent of their mirth is panic.

You are too old, Auguste, and show it,
It was not only Noah survived the flood.
You are too big and you should know it—
Your sawdust shadow shades the blood.
At midnight king's and hermit's mood
Heats from your small sad barbs that fester.
Your little dog is comic food,
Frankfurters for the giant deathless jester.

Isn't your circuit of the tent enough?
The child may find you in the meadow.
Your circuit of the tent is not enough.
White doppelganger, cruciform and narrow,
You scatter by your clownish shadow
Our dubious pigeons
                        home to roost,
                                august
                                    Auguste.

CLOWNS' SONGS

Sang Charlie, I cannot learn
If I am beautiful or not.
My glass has a crack.
He sang, The chestnuts burn
More hotly than I thought,
My blistered paw is black—
       Sang Charlie the clown.

Joey sang, My trapeze is flown
Like a bird and left me silly
And I slip, and flip
Down
      down
          down
Smack on my belly
In the net and up—
      Sang Joey the clown.

Sang Auguste, At midnight quite alone
Light the white light above the mirror;
My mask's big cliché—
The lips turned up or down—
(Is it the glass's error?)
Has nothing to say,
      Sang Auguste the clown.

The Minor Poet

The minor poet sits at meat
with danger smoldering in his eye,
to left, to right, his dicta fly,
impaling those who blot or botch:
should any dolt essay reply
his voice goes up another notch.

Attempts to qualify are doomed.
Who could object? Which would displease?
With finger raised, in tones that freeze
he checks his points: 1, 2, 3, 4.
By salad time, the very cheese
is paler, for his scorn and lore.

Wit dies before his massy frown—
until, bethinking, from his files
he fetches forth a *mot*, and smiles!
And not a man or woman weeps,
though each one knows that we have miles
and miles to go before he sleeps.

Birdsong of the Lesser Poet

Exuding someone's Scotch in a moving mist,
abstracted as he broods upon that grant,
he has an intimate word for those who might assist;
for a bad review, a memory to shame the elephant.

Who would unearth a mine, and fail to work it?
His erstwhile hosts are good for fun and games
that brighten the lumpen-audience on the poetry circuit.
He drops only the most unbreakable names.

Disguised as youth, he can assign all guilt;
his clothes proclaim a sort of permanent stasis.
With a hawk's eye for signs of professional wilt,
he weeds his garden of friends on a monthly basis.

And yet, and yet, to that unattractive head,
and yet, and yet, to that careful, cagey face,
comes now and again the true terrible word;
unearned, the brief visa into some state of grace.

Mr. Mahoney

Illicitly, Mr. Mahoney roams.
They have him in a room, but it is not his.
Though he has become confused, it is not in this.
Mr. Mahoney cannot find his room.

A young blond nurse gentles him by the elbow.
I hear her again in the hall: "Mr. Mahoney,
this isn't your room. Let's go back and see
if you've brushed your teeth. Yours is 820."

Why brushing his teeth is the lure, I cannot say.
Does he prize it so? She darts on white feet
to spear him from strange doors; I hear her repeat
with an angel's patience, "Yours is down *this* way."

But 820 is a swamp, a blasted heath.
A dozen times returned, he knows it is wrong.
There is a room in which he does belong.
He has been to 820; he has brushed his teeth.

Before his biopsy, the harried nurses attest,
Mr. Mahoney was tractable in 820,
though very old and brown. He will have to go;
that is not the hall, not the building for his quest.

Tranquilized, Mr. Mahoney still eludes.
At 2 A.M. in my dark 283
the wide door cracks, and sudden and silently
Mr. Mahoney's nutty face obtrudes.

It is gently snatched back by someone behind it.
"That is someone *else's* room. Yours is this way,
Mr. Mahoney." He could not possibly stay.
He is gone by noon. He did not have time to find it.

Survivor's Ballad

She's not sure if it's song or sermon,
ballad of a tightknit trio:
graduates of the Monday German,
two with beauty, and three with brio.

Three were cocky and three were witty;
two took a dim view of their local past or
future, took both to New York City.
But three times a year, they lunched at the Astor,

close as thieves in their favorite venue.
The waiter welcomed his favorite trio,
pink carnations and shiny menu;
two with beauty, and three with brio.

That was long before the trouble—
trio, carnations, wine and waiter.
The Hotel Astor has long been rubble,
she doesn't know what was built there later.

The beauties fought, and made it up;
but after that, it was *sauve qui peut*,
with more sharp cracks than a broken cup
and she ended with double lunches *à deux*.

The dark-eyed one was put through paces
by bitter pain before she went.
The blue-eyed one lost names, then faces,
then who she was and what she meant.

Song or sermon, poet or pastor,
a dream revisits the last of the trio:
greedy and young, at the Hotel Astor,
two with beauty, and three with brio.

You Can Take It with You

for Evelyn Prettyman

2 little girls who live next door
to this house are on their trampoline.
The window is closed, so they are soundless.

The sun slants, it is going away:
but now it hits full on the trampoline
and the small figure at each end.

Alternately they fly up to the sun,
fly, and rebound, fly, are shot
up, fly, are shot up up.

One comes down in the lotus
position. The other, outdone,
somersaults in air. Their hair

flies too. Nothing, nothing, noth-
ing can keep them down. The air
sucks them up by the hair of their heads.

I know all about what is
happening in this city at just
this moment; every last

grain of dark, I conceive.
But what I see now is:
the 2 little girls flung up

flung up, the sun snatch-
ing them, their mouths rounded
in gasps. They are there, they fly up.

The Blue-Eyed Exterminator

The exterminator has arrived. He has not intruded. He
    was summoned.
At the most fruitless spot, a regiment
of the tiniest of ants, obviously deluded,
have a jetty ferment of undisclosed intent.

The blue-eyed exterminator is friendly and fair;
one can tell he knows exactly what he is about.
He is young as the day that makes the buds puff out,
grass go rampant, big bees ride the air;

it seems the spring could drown him in its flood.
But though he appears modest as what he was summoned
    for,
he will prove himself more potent than grass or bud,
being a scion of the greatest emperor.

His success is total: no jet platoon on the wall.
At the door he calls good-bye and hitches his thumb.
For an invisible flick, grass halts, buds cramp, bees stall
in air. He has called, and what has been called has come.

X. J. KENNEDY

FROM

Dark Horses

1992

Woman in Rain

Down brimming streets she walks, the bole
Of a young tree uprooted whole,
     Impelled along a breakneck flood
     Of rushing traffic, flesh and blood.

Sleek taxis on the prowl for cash
Through overflowing potholes bash—
     She dodges sheets of water, steps
     Past handbills (DEEP MASSAGE—TRY SHEP'S)

And, twained by her determined stride,
The strings of rain to strands divide,
     A beaded curtain, thin and blue.
     She parts its danglings, steps on through

To farther rooms, still unaware
That she as we behold her there
     Might grace a page or fill a frame.
     But then, what planet knows its name?

Twelve Dead, Hundreds Homeless

The wind last night kept breaking into song—
Not a song, though, to comfort children by.
It picked up houses, flung them down awry,
Upended bridges, drove slow trees along
To walls.
        A note so high
Removed an ear that listened. On the strand
Without a word this morning, sailors land.
White cars, their sirens off, wade silently.

Now crews inch by, restringing power lines,
Plowing aside the sparkling drifts of glass.
The wind last night kept breaking into song
Beautiful only if you heard it wrong.

Veterinarian

Terrified bleat, bellow and hoofbeat, thrash,
She quiets with a black bag. Working alone
On hands and knees, a carpenter of flesh,
She joins together staves of broken bone,
Mends fences for the bloodstream that would run
Out of the raving dog, the shattered horse,
Her hands as sure as planets in their course.

Now prestidigitates before the wide-
Eyed children without trying to, intent
On tugging forth a live calf from the bride
Of the bull, bandages the brood mare's ligament.
Now by her labor arteries are bent,
Grappled, tied fast like saplings under duress.
She murmurs words to soothe the languageless.

Leaves like a plowman order in her wake.
Home for a hot tub and a single feast
Of last night's pizza, watching cold dawn break,
Knowing that some will live—a few, at least—
Though foam-jawed, wild-eyed, the eternal beast
Annihilation with perpetual neigh
Takes worlds like ours with water twice a day.

The Animals You Eat

The animals you eat
Leave footprints in your eyes.
You stare, four-year-old pools
Troubled. "They don't have souls,"
I tell you, in defeat.

Has no one ever dined
In bedtime stories pink
Cuddlable pigs inhabit,
No one stewed Peter Rabbit
In that land of pure mind?

You tinker with your burger,
Doubtful. "It doesn't matter,"
I say. We kill by proxy
And so, like Foxy Loxy,
Dissemble while we murder.

"Lambs wouldn't have a life
Romping in black-eyed Susans
If they weren't to be eaten."
But your lip quivers. Beaten,
I'm caught with dripping knife.

To bed now. Gravely wise,
You face night on your own.
I smooth your pillow and sheet.
The animals you eat
Start turning to your eyes.

On Being Accused of Wit

No, I am witless. Often in despair
At long-worked botches crumpled, thrown away—
A few lines worth the keeping, all too rare.
Blind chance not wit entices words to stay
And recognizing luck is artifice
That comes unlearned. The rest is taking pride
In daily labor. This and only this.
On keyboards sweat alone makes fingers glide.

Witless, that juggler rich in discipline
Who brought the Christchild all he had for gift,
Flat on his back with beatific grin
Keeping six slow-revolving balls aloft;
Witless, La Tour, that painter none too bright,
His draftsman's compass waiting in the wings,
Measuring how a lantern stages light
Until a dark room overflows with rings.

Ambition

First blow of October, and oak leaves shy
Down from branches they value not overly high
As though to cast off at a breath of cold
Were as easy as hanging on, gathering gold.

Their casualness ravishes. Was I wrong
To have clung to my workdesk the summer long,
Scratching out, striving? What now to show
But dread of the coming of drifted snow?

I'd be glad to go out on a limb with those
Who can live with whatever the wind bestows
Were it not for these roots, dug in deep to bear
Never being done grasping for light and air.

The Lords of Misrule

Jimmy Harlow

My third-best friend in grade school, Jimmy Harlow,
Like some shy twitch-nosed hare
Yearning to quit its burrow,
By teacher's harsh words once reduced to tears—
That day when, nine, you charged across the street
Not reckoning the car you'd meet by chance,
You stained a blanket thrown
To swerve the snowflakes from your broken bones.
You whined there, waiting for the ambulance.

After the accident
You lived just four more years,
Your skull crushed oblong, frail,
Face ashen-pale
And graven with an ineradicable squint.

I saw you last
At a New Year's party, locked in fierce embrace
With the loveliest girl in the place,
Dredging her with your sharp-chinned corpse-gray head.
I was aghast.
By April you were dead.

Lie in the ease of winter, Jimmy Harlow.
If I begrudged you her, I do not now.

Death of a First Child

in memory of M.J.G.

Christmas. The laden sack
　　Draws noose-tight now its string,
The cherished gift sent back
　　Though heralds sing,

Though tinkling carols drift
　　And dull-tongued church bells toll,
An anti-gift is left
　　Like stocking coal.

This year it seems not right
　　To mouth old words of joy,
Bless the blind world, or light
　　Candles without you, boy.

However brief, your fire
　　Like a clear amber shone.
Your grieving dam and sire
　　Shoulder a ton of stone.

I charge your spirit now:
　　Although a searing blast
Of winter smote your bough,
　　Be not the last

But one day harbinge in
　　A further host, good son,
Of your deserving kin.
　　Then you shall have begun

The raising of a house
   Beneath whose roof you fell.
In time your parents shall rejoice
   That in you they built well.

A Curse on a Thief

Paul Dempster had a handsome tackle box
In which he'd stored up gems for twenty years:
Hooks marvelously sharp, ingenious lures
Jointed to look alive. He went to Fox

Lake, placed it on his dock, went in and poured
Himself a frosty Coors, returned to find
Some craven sneak had stolen in behind
His back and crooked his entire treasure horde.

Bad cess upon the bastard! May the bass
He catches with Paul Dempster's pilfered gear
Jump from his creel, make haste for his bare rear,
And, fins outthrust, slide up his underpass.

May each ill-gotten catfish in his pan
Sizzle his lips and peel away the skin.
May every perch his pilfered lines reel in
Oblige him to spend decades on the can.

May he be made to munch a pickerel raw,
Its steely gaze fixed on him as he chews,
Choking on every bite, while metal screws
Inexorably lock his lower jaw,

And having eaten, may he be transformed
Into a trout himself, with gills and scales,
A stupid gasper that a hook impales,
In Hell's hot griddle may he be well warmed

And served with shots of lava on the rocks
To shrieking imps indifferent to his moans
Who'll rend his flesh and pick apart his bones,
Poor fish who hooked Paul Dempster's tackle box.

Maples in January

for Edgar Bowers

By gust and gale brought down to this
    Simplicity, they stand unleaved
    And momentarily reprieved
From preening photosynthesis.

Abandoned, tons of greenery.
    As though scorched bare by forest fire,
    They've shrugged the rustle of desire,
The chore of being scenery,

And now impervious to thirst,
    No longer thrall to summer's sway,
    They stand their ground as if to say,
Winter and wind, come do your worst.

CHARLES MARTIN

FROM   1987
Steal the Bacon

A Burial at Shanidar

Men of our kind, digging in the cellar
Of a cave, uncovered what was hidden:
Bones that from steeping in the earth's strong tea
For countless years had taken on its color.
But were those bones just tossed onto the midden,
Or had they been buried? A mystery.
The soiled fragments of a salvaged skull
At first said nothing but Neanderthal.

Bones in better repair, appearing beneath
That skull's dyed egg, allowed them to recover
A specimen long crippled by disease,
Worn out at forty, arthritic since his birth,
A burden on the group, which had, however,
Provided him with his necessities,
And afterwards had buried him and mourned,
With ceremony—as our cave men learned.

For when they sent the matter of that site
To be examined by a botanist
In Europe, she immediately found
The remnants of a grave—a shallow pit
Lined with pine branches, on which he'd been placed,
Before the group had scattered all around
What never could have gotten there by chance:
Cornflowers, hollyhock, grape-hyacinth.
Their custom noted in the dried-out pollen
Of long gone flowers, dropped by hands the same,
As fleeting as the shadows on the wall
That flickered in firelight around the fallen;
How hesitantly, awkwardly they came

Forward to celebrate his funeral,
Those dim, unsightly ancestors of ours,
Clutching their little sprays of wildflowers

And uttering their almost human cries
Of unsuccess, as shambling, grotesque,
They stood around the figure in the grave
And mumbled what might have meant, *Take these,*
Which we have gathered at no little risk
In the wild places far beyond the cave.
We thought to honor you. The reasons why
Would perish with the last of them to die.

E.S.L.

My frowning students carve
Me monsters out of prose:
This one—a gargoyle—thumbs its contemptuous nose
At how, in English, subject must agree
With verb—for any such agreement shows
    Too great a willingness to serve,
            A docility

    Which wiry Miss Choi
    Finds un-American.
She steals a hard look at me. I wink. Her grin
Is my reward. *In his will, our peace, our Pass*:
Gargoyle erased, subject and verb now in
    Agreement, reach object, enjoy
            Temporary truce.

    Tonight my students must
    Agree or disagree:
America is still a land of opportunity.
The answer is always, uniformly, *Yes*—even though
"It has no doubt that here were to much free,"
    As Miss Torrico will insist.
            She and I both know

    That Language binds us fast,
    And those of us without
Are bound and gagged by those within. Each fledgling
        polyglot
Must shake old habits: tapping her sneakered feet,
Miss Choi exorcises incensed ancestors, flout-
    ing the ghosts of her Chinese past.
            Writing in the seat

Next to Miss Choi, Mister
Fedakis, in anguish
Labors to express himself in a tongue which
Proves *Linear B* to me, when I attempt to read it
Later. They're here for English as a Second Language,
    Which I'm teaching this semester.
            God knows they need it,

And so, thank God, do they.
    The night's made easier
By our agreement: I am here to help deliver
Them into the good life they write me papers about.
English is pre-requisite for that endeavor,
    Explored in their nightly essays
            Boldly setting out

To reconnoiter the fair
    New World they would enter:
Suburban Paradise, the endless shopping center
Where one may browse for hours before one chooses
Some new necessity—gold-flecked magenta
    Wallpaper to re-do the spare
            Bath no one uses,

Or a machine which can,
    In seven seconds, crush
A newborn calf into such seamless mush
As a *mousse* might be made of—or our true sublime:
The gleaming counters where frosted cosmeticians brush
    Decades from the allotted span,
            Abrogating Time

As the spring tide brushes
A single sinister
Footprint from the otherwise unwrinkled shore
Of America the Blank. In absolute confusion
Poor Mister Fedakis rumbles with despair
And puts the finishing smutches
To his conclusion

While Miss Choi erases:
One more gargoyle routed.
Their pure, erroneous lines yield an illuminated
Map of the new found land. We will never arrive there,
Since it exists only in what we say about it,
As all the rest of my class is
Bound to discover.

Making Faces

for Peter Schumann

We begin to see that it is better to keep life fluid and
changing than to try to hold it down fast in heavy
monuments. . . . Give us things that are alive and flexible,
which won't last too long and become an obstruction and a
weariness.

D. H. LAWRENCE

I   THE WORLD

Every year there is a big parade
In Barton, Vermont, on the Fourth of July
When we celebrate the red white and blue—
During the course of which we see displayed
Some of the Pentagon's old weaponry;
An armored car, a Sherman tank or two
Add martial tone to the festive atmosphere:
Behind them come the Bread & Puppet Theatre,
Beginning with someone in a horse's head
Who's holding up a sign which says, THE WORLD,
As though the world were next in their procession,
Or their procession were the world instead.
And next to the horse there walks a little girl
Ringing a schoolbell for our attention:

The world we see approaching is a cart
Drawn by puppet oxen, their huge necks bent,
Their tranquil heads sweeping from side to side;
The world is filled with artless works of art,

Miniature figures that must represent
The people of the world out for a ride.
And the cart so full of them that one might say
No one at all has been left home today.
The world has drawn beside us now and soon
Will pass us by as the clouds pass us by
Overhead. The clouds move at their own pace
And so to us they hardly seem to move,
Those ghostly, gray-white oxen of the sky
Drawing the world through realms of empty space.

This world addresses the fragility
Of the only other one we have to live in,
Where the marble-breasted laborers grow weak
And stumble to their knees and shortly die;
Where the poor must eat the stones that they are given
And the little painted figures fall and break;
And the extraordinary cloud-drawn cart
We thought would last forever comes apart.
What happens next in the parade, we ask?
We haven't long to wait before our answer:
Behind the cart drawn by the puppet oxen
Comes a stilted figure in a jackal's mask,
Pounding on a drum! This dog-faced dancer
Raises a clangorous, dissonant tocsin:

II   THE END OF THE WORLD

We've practiced it too often in our age
To see it merely as the subtraction
Of bird from tree, of tree from earth, of earth from space,
As one erases letters from a page.
Yet we still think of it as an abstraction,
Something that isn't likely to take place—
Although it's taken place at places called

Guernica, Hiroshima, Buchenwald.
We think of the unthinkable with ease,
We've had such practice of it for so long;
And speak of it in ways which help conceal
From ourselves the dark realities
That numb the mind and paralyze the tongue.
And now in the parade there comes a skel-

etal figure on a skeletal horse,
Made of raw strips of pine lashed together.
Its attitude is distant yet familiar,
As though it were confident that in the course
Of time we'd get to know each other better.
It knows this in its bones, as we in ours.
(And so if Death should ever wave at you,
You may wave back, for you have manners too;
You needn't ask it to slow down or stop.)
It's followed by a Dragon, belching smoke;
One Demon drives it, another one attends
To the Great Devourer who sits on top,
Quietly enjoying some huge cosmic joke—
And that is the way The End Of The World ends.

III   FIGHT THE END OF THE WORLD

Now Peter Schumann, dressed as Uncle Sam,
Strides down Main Street on his outrageous stilts
Carrying a sign that says, WATCH OUT!
A younger Uncle Sam prances around him,
Intricately weaving subtle steps
Under his teacher's exaggerated strut—
"They make it looks so easy," someone says.
They dance before a ragtime band which plays
Molto con brio, more or less on key;

For there are many fine musicians in it
And they raise a joyful noise unto the Lord
Of all creation. The heart willingly
Gives its assent, but mind says, Wait a minute—
Is this how we're to Fight The End Of The World?

—By making faces at appalling forces
And marching off to the Parade Grounds with
One's friends and neighbors, honest country folk
Changed into demons, dogs and demi-horses,
Or into oxen who present the world as myth,
Straining together underneath their yoke?
—By building things so that they cannot last
Unreasonably long? By honoring the past,
But raising up no wearisome immense
Rock for all ages? By rudely waking
The child-in-us and teaching it to play?
By going with the grain and not against?
By shaping our daily bread and baking
Thick-crusted loaves of it to give away?

We've seen The World as it was passing through,
And monstrous Death the world-devouring,
And a man on stilts, whose artistry astounded;
And now we have a sanitation crew
Sweeping and shoveling up dragon dung,
Leaving the street as spotless as they'd found it.
My questions beg an answer, as do I.
Some kind of answer may be given by
The Garbageman who shakes hands with my son
And daughter, then goes back to join his friends;
Or the Washerwoman in her faded dress,
On a holiday from work that's never done,
With whom, most fittingly, the pageant ends:
As she passes by, her sign says only, YES

What the Darkness Proposes

Flying Heads

Lopped off, they jetted wings at shoulder level
A moment after their brief lives were ended;
Skittering from the clutches of the Devil,
The little ones ascended

In formation to surround Our Savior
And fan the victors of the Church Triumphant.
Cited on the field for good behavior,
Each newly halo'd infant

Fusses and fidgets, waiting for the Day
Of Judgment, when the dead will all be sifted,
And those who've been naughty will be led away
While the righteous are uplifted . . .

Artists would afterwards enjoy devising
Improvements on that model—if a second
Pair of wings would aid in stabilizing
Erratic flybabies, they reckoned

That a third pair would be even better:
Two wings prone, two supine, two akimbo,
According to the spirit or the letter
Of the law in Limbo,

Where some had been consigned by their Creator.
In Limbo is Latin, meaning *on the border:*
There, tiny passengers whose elevator
Has gone out of order

Wait between floors now on their way to heaven:
Some pressing noses against the emergency button,
Some hanging upside down like bats in a cavern—
Not remembered, not forgotten.

Stanzas after *Endgame*

1/

Hurrying toward a tiny Off-Off-Off-
Off-Broadway theatre on the Bowery,
We step around a shouting match of gruff
    Derelicts whose poverty
This Sunday afternoon has found a small
Stage to enact its outrage on, a temporary
    Refuge from the wrecker's ball;

2/

Here artists and their lofts survive by grace
Of our needy city's celebrated
Developers, whose greed for office space
    Seems for now to have abated;
And here men wait with rags and dirty water
To smear new grime on windshields of intimidated
    Drivers who curse, but give a quarter;

3/

Quarters accumulated buy a quart
Of *Gold Coin Extra* or *Lone Star Malt Brew*;
Others do crack or heroin, or snort
    Fumes out of bags of plastic glue;
In the urinous storefronts where they meet,
Nodding acquaintances impatiently renew
    The ties that bind them to the street.

4/

No better place than this to stage a play
That illustrates the way the world will end,
For who will come to see it anyway,

But the subscribers, who attend
Everything? Yet look: pressed against the curb's
Split lip, twin arks—from which, in disbelief descend
Dazed voyagers from distant suburbs:

5/

Two *Short Line* buses with the audience:
The first is full of high school kids and teachers,
The second carries senior citizens
Clutching discount ticket vouchers;
As they negotiate from stairs and aisle,
Purplespiked mutants grimly stalk the blue-rinsed grouches
Up and into the theater, while

6/

We in the middle find our seats and pray,
Unhopefully, that Beckett's spare precision
Survive all cries of "What did he just say?"
And adolescent snorts of derision:
The young with their tongues in one anothers' ears,
And their elders talking back to television,
Except this isn't television, dears.

7/

The lights go down and we become aware
Of someone on stage, motionless at first,
Beginning to move around a covered chair;
The way taken is at once reversed:
Upstage, downstage, dithering left and right,
Until the tiny stage is thoroughly traversed:
No other characters in sight.

8/

A promising beginning this is not.
From a few rows back comes an angry hiss:
"Isn't it . . . doesn't it . . . hasn't it . . . got a plot?"
      An answer started from across
The aisle is throttled down in someone's throat as
We lean into a vortex of expanding loss,
      That's taken us before we notice;

9/

New characters emerge, the sum of their
Seemingly irreversible reverses:
Hamm (underneath the covers on the chair)
      Joins *Clov* (on stage) and fiercely curses
Progenitor and Genetrix (the droll
Nagg, the winsome *Nell*) then brokenly rehearses
      Life at ground zero of the soul,

10/

Where first there is not enough and then there's more
And more of not enough, insufficiency
In slow addition, grain upon grain before
      It happens ever so suddenly
That insufficiency becomes too much
To bear, absent the hope that there might ever be
      Enough insufficiency, as such.

11/

Once there was something other than what's here,
Which is to say, a time that wasn't now:
Once shape and shapeless played with far and near,
      Motion and stillness, brightness and shadow;
Once there were places variously green
And pools they had, of clear water, wherein we saw
      Ourselves and our selves were seen—

12/

Reflections and expansions of the self!
The past not merely an accumulation!
Progressive toys on every kiddie's shelf!
        —But why must we go on and on
About the something more than not enough?
No reason: even as insufficiency, redun-
        dancy, though made of sterner stuff,

13/

Is certainly as equally absurd,
Meaningless, purposeless—yet we attend,
Hang, it is fair to say, on every word
        That brings us nearer to the end
Of stillness and silence. A brief tableau,
Then darkness separates those who must stay behind
        From those who are now free to go.

14/

From this immersion we emerge subdued
And seem more careful of one another;
The elders less cranky and the young not rude
        But helpful as we leave together,
Guiding an elbow, retrieving a dropped cane
For someone old enough to be Adam's grandfather,
        And whom we'll never meet again.

15/

Why are we so changed? Perhaps it's simple:
A parable of Kafka's comes to mind,
Of the leopards who break into the temple
        And drink the spirits that they find
In consecrated vessels; their continual
Thefts (being now predictable) are soon assigned
        A part within the ritual.

16/

Meaning emerges out of random act
And lasts as long as there are those intent
On finding it and keeping it intact
     In fables of impermanence.
We leave the theater as though illustrating
How hard that is to do. The going audience
     Begins to board the buses waiting

17/

At curbside to recall them from this dream
Into their lives: the young are making dates,
Their elders trying to remember them.
     Slowly, slowly, it separates!
Some are still standing outside the theater,
While others take off briskly down the darkening streets
     Wrapped up in their own thought, or

18/

Arguing, like these four on the corner,
About the meaning of it all, before
They set out to find themselves some dinner
     At the newly redecorated Hunan Court,
Where many fragrant wonders are provided
Soon for the delectation of one carnivore,
     Two vegetarians, one undecided.

ROBERT PACK

FROM   1980

Waking to My Name

Departing Words to a Son

We choose to say goodbye against our will
Home will take on stillness when you're gone
Remember us—but don't dwell on the past
Here—wear this watch my father gave to me

Home will take on stillness when you're gone
We'll leave your room as is—at least for now
Here—wear this watch my father gave to me
His face dissolves within the whirling snow

We'll leave your room as is—at least for now
I'll dust the model boats that sail your wall
His face dissolves within the whirling snow
It's hard to picture someone else's life

I'll dust the model boats that sail your wall
Don't lose the watch—the inside is engraved
It's hard to picture someone else's life
Your window's full of icicles again

Don't lose the watch—the inside is engraved
A wedge of geese heads somewhere out of sight
Your window's full of icicles again
Look how the icicles reflect the moon

A wedge of geese heads somewhere out of sight
My father knew the distances we keep
Look how the icicles reflect the moon
The moonlight shimmers wave-like on your wall

My father knew the distances we keep
Your mother sometimes cries out in the night
The moonlight shimmers wave-like on your wall
One June I dove too deep and nearly drowned

Your mother sometimes cries out in the night
She dreams the windy snow has covered her
One June I dove too deep and nearly drowned
She says she's watched me shudder in my sleep

She dreams the windy snow has covered her
She's heard your lost scream stretch across the snow
She says she's watched me shudder in my sleep
We all conceive the loss of what we love

She's heard your lost scream stretch across the snow
My need for her clenched tighter at your birth
We all conceive the loss of what we love
Our love for you has given this house breath

My need for her clenched tighter at your birth
Stillness deepens pulsing in our veins
Our love for you has given this house breath
Some day you'll pass this watch on to your son

Stillness deepens pulsing in our veins
My father's words still speak out from the watch
Some day you'll pass this watch on to your son
Repeating what the goldsmith has etched there

My father's words still speak out from the watch
As moonlit icicles drip on your sill
Repeating what the goldsmith has etched there
We choose to say goodbye against our will.

A Modest Boast at Meridian

No spring can follow past meridian

STEVENS

If I embraced a horse, baby,
with all my power,
its neck would stretch like a giraffe's
in one impassioned hour;
and if I nibbled your ear,
an elephant, trumpeting its charge,
would thunder through the forest
of your veins at large.
Take me, my girl,
at the least pleading, I am your own,
prepared to spread largesse among all beasts
who famish at the bone
and wish to freshen at my watering place
where bannered leaves parade the wind's reply:
Be fruitful and go multiply!
Honey, by God, I vow the rains
will swell your lettuce-patch;
the hens will chortle in their huts,
and every golden egg will hatch.
And if, poor mortal girl, the truth
is all that we can bear,
I swear that I'll concoct a yarn
for us to weave our winter bed in
now that lying youth is gone.

The Shooting

I shot an otter because I had a gun;
The gun was loaned to me, you understand.
Perhaps I shot it merely for the fun.
Must everything have meaning and be planned?

Afterwards I suffered penitence,
And dreamed my dachshund died, convulsed in fright.
They look alike, but that's coincidence.
Within one week my dream was proven right.

At first I thought its death significant
As punishment for what I'd lightly done;
But good sense said I'd nothing to repent,
That it is natural to hunt for fun.

Was I unnatural to feel remorse?
I mourned the otter and my dog as one.
But superstition would not guide my course;
To prove that I was free I bought the gun.

I dreamed I watched my frightened brother die.
Such fancy worried me, I must admit.
But at his funeral I would not cry,
Certain that I was not to blame for it.

I gave my friend the gun because of guilt,
And feared then what my sanity had done.
On fear, he said, the myth of hell was built.
He shot an otter because he had a gun.

Raking Leaves

Packed with woodpeckers, my head knocks,
Coaxing the bark of the tree to make its sap speak—
My sap, my boned branches, my veined leaves
Staining the wind, dizzying down
Amid a busyness of birds.

And in the bedroom, flushed hands warm with work,
She smoothes the wrinkles from the sheets
That last night's tumbled sleep may once again
Grow young, that habit, fondled back
Into desire, may heat the holy place
Where flesh is sung. And unknown even
To herself—who does not live by words—
She dreams this place again, again,
Whose branches are the memories of birds;
She eases drifting through a noon of bells
Replenishing her purpose to return,
With no debts in her comings or farewells.

Raking, quickly taking time in the nick,
I watch my feet glide through the ragged shade
Of the shagbark hickory, burly in the blood
Of my own speed, my own strength, now smack
In the sun, savagely bright, sight
For closed eyes; and up, out again to seek,
I take, I make what I will, skill of delight
I am not author of; above, no missing God I miss;
High satisfying sky though, and below,
Chrysanthemums in garb of gaiety,
Little serious clowns; and look, beyond the brook
The fat grouse bumps across the field
And jumps for berries in the honeysuckle.

Not here, not now, one world goes down,
And, not in my head, the serious men
Chronicle its going; I cannot tell them
I am raking leaves. This day is hers,
This is my time; with us together
Two chores away, all rocking hours support
This hour, all knocking days repeat this day.

In the Waking

In the waking of my eye
The ringing winter world runs white,
Two cardinals are points of light,
An icicle reflects the sky,
And snow-carved pines curve into sight.

But now the whiteness starts to blind,
And through a dark transparency
The winter morning murmury
With worlds to come wakes in my mind
A thought of you whose thought is me.

I cannot love myself alone,
Yet see you watching me apart,
And all my eye's spontaneous art
Is still as icicle and stone
And timeless as this planet's start.

You are the one I single out
To rouse my passive eye to dance
And make a choice where all is chance—
Of stars exploding in the night
Whose lost lights endlessly advance.

A Cage in Search of a Bird

My destiny is not my own
Said the cage in search of a bird.
I am defined by what I do,
And when I'm empty, I'm absurd.

So I will find a willing bird
Who knows the limit of the skies
With wings that feel the chain his song
Must hold him in until he dies.

And he will make my bars his home
Beyond all vistas of the air,
And sing his song to me alone
Inside the echoes of despair.

And if some other bird should stop
When flying south to look and spin
About and say, "You can't get out,"
He would reply, "You can't get in."

A Bird in Search of a Cage

Said the bird in search of a cage:
This world is even large for wings,
The mindless seasons drive me down,
Tormenting me with changing things.

A cage is not escape, but need,
And though once in all travel's done,
I'll sing so every bird will know
My wanderings in moon and sun,

And all the crickets will be stilled,
And stilled the summer air and grass,
And hushed the secrets of the wind,
For when my final callings pass.

And if a friend should stop to talk,
Reminding me of what is past,
And ask the meaning of my song,
I'd say that only cages last.

ROBERT PHILLIPS

FROM   1994

Breakdown Lane

The Stone Crab: A Love Poem

*Joe's serves approximately 1000 pounds of crab claws
each day.*—Florida Gold Coast Leisure Guide

Delicacy of warm Florida waters,
his body is undesirable. One giant claw
is his claim to fame, and we claim it,

more than once. Meat sweeter than lobster,
less dear than his life, when grown that claw
is lifted, broken off at the joint.

Mutilated, the crustacean is thrown back
into the water, back upon his own resources.
One of nature's rarities, he replaces

an entire appendage as you or I
grow a nail. (No one asks how he survives
that crabby sea with just one claw;

two-fisted menaces real as night-
mares, ten-tentacled nights cold
as fright.) In time he grows another,

large, meaty, magnificent as the first.
And one astonished day, *snap!* it too
is twigged off, the cripple dropped

back into treachery. Unlike a twig,
it sprouts again. How many losses
can he endure? Well,

his shell is hard, the sea is wide.
Something vital broken off, he doesn't
nurse the wound; develops something new.

I Remember, I Remember

(poem beginning with two lines by Yehuda Amichai)

The earth drinks people and their loves
like wine, in order to forget.
But I drink wine to remember.

I remember the day at school I thought
I had appendicitis. My father came,
supported me on both sides to the car,

into the doctor's. For that, when Gabriel
blows his horn, may Father be supported
on both sides to Heaven.

I remember the sensation of first love,
like falling down a mine shaft.
But shafts are dark, and all around

me was light, light, light. Her hair
light, and when we locked together
we were a dynamo generating light.

I remember not knowing what I wanted to do
in life. My ambitions scattered like newspapers
on lawns of people out of town,

until I had the right professor for
the right course. Suddenly I was on course
for what I'd do until the day I die.

I remember the day we were wed. In early
morning I walked down Marshall Street,
wanted to proclaim to everyone I met,

"I'm marrying a woman who makes me laugh,
a beautiful woman good as fresh-baked bread,
pure as a beach where no one walks."

I remember the day our son was born,
the longest day and night and day
of my life—imagine how long for her!

When the nurse brought our son to the window,
I was Robinson Crusoe discovering Friday's
footprint: stranger, companion, friend.

I remember, sometimes more than I care to,
the friend I let down unintentionally,
the brothers I hurt through simple silence,

the mother I didn't call often enough when
she was bedridden, weak as water. I even
remember a dog who wanted to play. I didn't.

I remember the day it was confirmed
one of my friends had been telling
lies about me for years—

they cost me friends, a coveted job.
May his tongue be ripped out
and flung to the crows.

I collect memories the way some collect coins.
The memories fade like constellations at dawn.
Until my next glass of wine.

603 Cross River Road

for Judith

1972: The Land—A Love Letter

This hill and the old house on it
are all we have. Two acres
more or less—half crabby lawn,
half field we mow but twice a year.

Some trees we planted, most gifts
of the land. The pine by the kitchen?
Grown twice as fast as our son. The bald
elm lost the race with my hairline.

The mulberry—so lively with squirrels,
chipmunk chases, and songbirds—
fell like a tower in the hurricane.
My chainsaw ate fruitwood for weeks.

(I stacked the heavy logs by the cellar
door, to be retrieved winter nights
for the fireplace, not knowing it's easier
to burn a cement block than a mulberry.)

The juniper tree, the one that all but
obliterated our view? Men cut it down
to make way for the new well and water
pump. That pump should pump pure gold:

we lay awake engineering ways to get it
paid for. But we'll never leave
this mortgaged hill, we thought.
This land is changing as we change,

its face erodes like ours—weather marks,
stretch marks, traumas of all sorts
and conditions. Last night a limb broke
in the storm. We still see it limn the sky.

Wife, we've become where we have been.
This land is all we have, but this love
letter is no more ours than anyone's
who ever married the land . . .

1982: Autumn Crocuses

Basketing leaves during earth's
annual leavetaking, we've realized
with a start—something's missing.
The autumn crocuses that would spring

each October by these rocks.
No longer here! We never planted them,
but they implanted themselves
on us. Now, for their lack

we are poorer. Purest orchid color,
they astonished amidst the season's
dwindling. Crocus in autumn?
How perverse, to reverse the seasons.

Every year we bore a bouquet
into the house with pride,
surprising guests who'd never seen
their like. They thought them

foreign, remote, inaccessible—
like edelweiss. No vase, glass, or jar
ever contained them. Their soft white
stems always bent, jack-eared blossoms

lolled like heads of old folks
sleeping in rocking chairs.
I read once where their yellow pistils
are a saffron source. For us,

source of satisfaction. Now gone.
A woodchuck? Frost? My failure to care
for bulbs? They were the unaccountable
we thought we could count on.

1992: Farewell to the Blue House

Our favorite time of year was fall.
Autumn crocuses had blazed
in rock gardens like gas flames,
trees painted themselves pumpkin,
apple, fireplace smoke traveled

in the breezes. The fall of leaves
created a cinematic panorama—
the spangled lake blue, bluer
than blue beneath Westchester's
skies. Mornings, Canada geese

vectored down, honking and hunkering
in the lower field. Evenings, deer
leapt stone walls, drank their fill.
In the upper field, wild turkeys
strutted. The peaceable kingdom.

Whenever I tired of the city,
I lost myself in trees.
Whenever I tired of human faces,
I bent down sunflowers,
gazed into friendly countenances.

The sun setting over the reservoir,
orange overcoming bruise-colored clouds—
no one felt luckier to have landed somewhere.
Somedays I felt as if I could walk across that water.

FROM 1999

Unarmed and Dangerous

A Child's Christmas in Georgia, 1953

Marching through Georgia to bed, he stopped, listened,
And heard, "While shepherds washed their socks by
    night."
Later, he sang the same skewed line off key,
And his parents howled; until getting it wrong,
He decided, beat getting it right.

But Christmas Eve they read about killing
The first-born, fleeing the land, and returning
By another country, till he couldn't sleep
And had to check so slipped from bed to stare
The darkened height by which the wise men steered.

Downstairs there were his mother's stacks of albums
And, mantle-high, her unblinking gallery
Of gold-framed graybeards gazing, and matriarchs
In black, scowling the generations back
Into place; and then there were the others,

His infant older brother who never
Came home, two cousins lost in war, an uncle
Who captained his ship over the flat world's edge,
And one fleece-lined pilot lost years now inside
The stilled weather of a relative's box camera.

And then there were the lines he'd heard in church,
"Pray that your flight may not be in winter,"
So that was how the pilot disappeared?
And "Woe to the pregnant and nursing," so
That explained his brother, or their mother?

There was one thing he knew by heart by now:
Rubella cooked, cleaned, and scolded her way
Through the house tuning the news and talking back,
Though she didn't vote, and said her baby
Died because he wouldn't come out in Georgia.

Still standing there and staring up, he pressed
His face till the cold glass fogged and hurt his nose,
Though there was only the street light yellowing
The side yard and his father's dormant garden
And the Talmadges' coiled drive and empty house.

So what were they singing about, the records
And radio? And why all these presents
When over drinks his parents grieved those missing?
What was given if you had to go away
And wound up framed like a silent question?

In the morning Rubella would light the stove;
The paper boy would whistle up Milledge,
Tossing the new day high over one hedge
Into another by the porch for parents
Who ignored their food and read to themselves.

So, still at the window, he studied the sky,
Figuring Pontius Pilate flew for Delta
And that the two parts to the Bible were
The Old and New Estimates, which like Christmas
You read out of the names of those missing.

Haying

They are gathering hay. The truck rolls slowly.
The men walk on either side, lifting bales,
Talking without looking up. When one truck fills
Another takes its place, the loaded truck
Turning for the barn, where another crew waits
To get the bales up to the loft.

                    There is a boy
They've hired for one day; he gets half wages.
They've put him at the top where it's hot,
Where he drags the bales from the lazy belt.
He can't lift the bales, so he backs then tugs,
Backs then tugs, feeling the barn's tin roof bake down.

They've worked since 6 A.M. and now the sun
Enlarges through the trees, which line the field's
Far edge, where the other crew follows a truck.
The older men wear overalls; the young men
Are stripped to the waist. The boy still wears his shirt.
Twice he has tried tobacco, twice gotten sick,
But now he is tired and elated,
Seeing the field's last load turning towards the barn.

Then tugging a bale, he brushes the nest.
And there are yellow jackets everywhere.
And the stings are everywhere, under his shirt,
On his ears, down each arm, and he is running,
Tripping, stung, running again, stung, climbing
Through the stings and rolling along the loft,
Another sting, and the loft's floor opening

And he sees the battered truck, the men circled
And he is on the truck's bed looking up,
The men still circled, and gazing down.
They don't move him, they will not move him,
And he can't move himself.
                              Old Smythe bends near
And puts tobacco on the stings.
He breaks a cigarette, chews the tobacco,
Then puts it on a sting—here, there, another . . .
Then another cigarette.
                         He asks the boy
Can he move his legs. The boy says, no,
Yes, maybe . . . maybe in a minute.

The men talk on, as calmly as before—
Complain about the heat, swat flies, light up.
The doctor's on his way and it's all right
Because they meant to quit, needed to,
Else they would have started the next field
And never gotten home.
                          Lie there, boy,
And listen to their neutral voices—
Used for selecting seed, planting, calving,
Used when wringing necks or cutting calves to steers,
Used for harvest, slaughter, funerals, drought—
And August always turns to drought,
One baking gust that cures the grass
Like a breath inhaled and held
So long that light turns colors.

The Ferris Wheel

The rounding steeps and jostles were one thing;
And he held tight with so much circling.
The pancaked earth came magnifying up,
Then shrank, as climbing backward to the top
He looked ahead for something in the fields
To stabilize the wheel.

Sometimes it stopped. The chairs rocked back and forth,
As couples holding hands got off
And others climbed into the empty chairs;
Then they were turning, singles, pairs,
Rising, falling through everything they saw,
Whatever thing they saw.

Below—the crowd, a holiday of shirts,
Straw hats, balloons, and brightly colored skirts,
So beautiful, he thought, looking down now,
While the stubborn wheel ground on, as to allow
Some stark monotony within,
For those festooned along the rim.

The engine, axle, spokes, and gears were rigged
So at the top the chairs danced tipsy jigs,
A teetering both balanced and extreme,
"Oh no," the couples cried, laughing, "Stop!" they screamed
Over the rounding down they rode along,
Centrifugal and holding on.

And he held too, thinking maybe happiness
Was simply going on, kept up unless
The wheel slowed or stopped for good. Otherwise,
There were the voices, expectant of surprise;
Funny to hear, he thought, their cries, always late,
Each time the wheel would hesitate,

Since the genius of the wheel was accident,
The always-almost that hadn't,
A minor agony rehearsed as fun
While the lights came up and dark replaced the sun,
Seeming to complete their going round all day,
Paying to be turned that way.

Later, standing off, he felt the wheel's mild dread,
Going as though it lapped the miles ahead
And rolled them up into the cloudless black,
While those who rode accelerated back
And up into the night's steep zero-G
That proved them free.

Elderly Lady Crossing on Green

And give her no scouts doing their one good deed
Or sentimental cards to wish her well
During Christmas time or gallstone time—
Because there was a time, she'd like to tell,

She drove a loaded V8 powerglide
And would have run you flat as paint
To make the light before it turned on her,
Make it as she watched you faint

When looking up you saw her bearing down
Eyes locking you between the wheel and dash,
And you either scrambled back where you belonged
Or jaywalked to eternity, blown out like trash

Behind the grease spot where she braked on you. . . .
Never widow, wife, mother, or a bride,
And nothing up ahead she's looking for
But asphalt, the dotted line, the other side,

The way she's done a million times before,
With nothing in her brief to tell you more
Than she's a small tug on the tidal swell
Of her own sustaining notion that she's doing well.

A Note of Thanks

Wallet stolen, so we must end our stay.
Then, while checking out, the wallet reappears
With an unsigned note saying, "Please forgive me;
This is an illness I have fought for years,
And for which you've suffered innocently.
P.S. I hope you haven't phoned about the cards."
I wave the wallet so my wife will see.
Smiling, she hangs up, and smiling she regards
The broad array of others passing by,
Each now special and uniquely understood.
We go back to our unmade room and laugh,
Happily agreeing that the names for "good"
Are not quite adequate and that each combines
Superlatives we but rarely think.
For the next three nights we drink a better wine.
And every day we go back through to check
The shops, buying what before had cost too much,
As if now Christmas and birthdays were planned
Years in advance. We watch others and are touched
To see how their faces are a dead-panned
Generality, holding close
The wishes and desires by which we all are gripped.
All charities seem practical to us,
All waiters deserving a bigger tip.
And, though we counter such an urge,
We start to think we'd like to meet the thief,
To shake the hand of self-reforming courage
That somehow censored a former disbelief.

Then we are home and leafing through the bills
Sent us from an unknown world of pleasure;
One of us likes cheap perfume; the other thrills

Over shoes, fedoras, expensive dinners;
There are massage parlors and videos,
Magazines, sunglasses, pharmaceuticals,
Long-distance calls, a host of curios,
Gallons of booze. . . . Only now we make our call.
But then, on hold, we go on sifting through
The mail till turning up a postcard view
Of our hotel. Flipping it and drawing blanks,
We read, "So much enjoyed my stay with you
I thought I ought to jot a note of thanks."

Balance as Belief

Learning the Bicycle

for Heather

The older children pedal past
Stable as little gyros, spinning hard
To supper, bath, and bed, until at last
We also quit, silent and tired
Beside the darkening yard where trees
Now shadow up instead of down.
Their predictable lengths can only tease
Her as, head lowered, she walks her bike alone
Somewhere between her wanting to ride
And her certainty she will always fall.

Tomorrow, though I will run behind,
Arms out to catch her, she'll tilt then balance wide
Of my reach, till distance makes her small,
Smaller, beyond the place I stop and know
That to teach her I had to follow
And when she learned I had to let her go.

What Women Know, What Men Believe

A Winter's Tale

for Ian

Silent and small in your wet sleep,
You grew to the traveler's tale
We made of you so we could keep
You safe in our vague pastoral,

And silent when the doctors tugged
Heels up your body free of its
Deep habitat, shoulders shrugged
Against the cold air's continent

We made you take for breathing.
Ian, your birth was my close land
Turned green, the stone rolled back for leaving,
My father dead and you returned.

GIBBONS RUARK

FROM   1983

Keeping Company

Watching You Sleep under Monet's Water Lilies

Beloved, you are sleeping still,
Your light grown rumpled where it fell,

You are sleeping under the dark
Of a down comforter. The heart

Of dawn light blooming on the wall
Has not yet touched you where you still

Lie breathing, though it has wakened
The faint lilies, strewn and broken

Cloud-lights littering the water.
That you breathe is all that matters,

That you keep breathing, lily,
While I wake to write this folly

Down, this breath of song that has your
Beauty lying among the pure

Lilies of the morning water,
Even though a light wind shatter

Them forever, and the too deep
Pool of desiring fill with sleep.

With Our Wives in Late October

for James Wright

Wandering with weather down the long hillside,
We come to the slender reeds in the water,
All of us who lazed by our own rivers
    Summer and autumn,

Looking for redwings or leaves that were falling,
Light that was flying, the red wing of summer,
Never dreaming to be by one sure river
    Gathered together.

Now by the slender reeds in the water
Annie and Kay are looking for spiders,
Their own thoughts slender as the thoughts of
   spiders
    Looking for women.

Diligent spiders are our kindred creatures,
Friends of the season, and they are raveling
Somewhere lonelier than I can follow
    With all my singing,

But here's one Annie has suddenly sighted
Loitering brightly over the water,
Letting his legged and delicate star-body
    Flash us a signal

Clearer than water or the redwing's shoulder:
Some stars in heaven already dying
Light up the moonless night that is coming,
    Some stars are other

Bodies altogether, reluctant to say
How they become the light of October,
This spider, these leaves, these loveliest
    Faces of women.

For the Pause before We Decorate the Tree

Dark pine tree hung with fragrance,
Your branches are all lit
With spiderwebs, small vagrants
Carrying light from twig

To twig, themselves the darkest
Stars I ever gazed on,
Vacant shinings like the points
Of some ghost constellation,

Its destinations darkened
But its ways still showing
Frail and luminous, broken
Light-net in the needles.

Dark pine tree light with spiders,
Stand there all afternoon
Lifting those fragrant branches
We will soon weigh down.

Dark pine tree beautifully
Dying into daylight,
Remind me late or early
How the evening gathers

Weight and gathers stillness
Till I lie down with her
And begin to touch her
In those places farther

From me sometimes than the stars
Are far from spiders
In your branches, than the years
Have fallen from her face.

I will kiss the good grave hollow
Between her breasts, her thin
Inner wrist, the cool shallow
Cup above her collar-bone,

All these and more, till near dawn
Light along her left wrist
Is a thread trembling from one place
Kissed to another kissed.

Dark pine tree hung with fragrance,
Are these scattered kisses
I imprint her with dark stars
Or simple darknesses?

Waiting for You with the Swallows

I was waiting for you
Where the four lanes wander
Into a city street,
Listening to the freight
Train's whistle and thunder
Come racketing through,

And I saw beyond black
Empty branches the light
Turn swiftly to a flurry
Of wingbeats in a hurry
For nowhere but the flight
From steeple-top and back

To steeple-top again.
I thought of how the quick
Hair shadows your lit face
Till laughter in your voice
Awoke and brought me back
And you stepped from the train.

I was waiting for you
Not a little too long
To learn what swallows said
Darkening overhead:
When we had time, we sang.
After we sang, we flew.

Words to Accompany a Leaf from the Great Copper Beech at Coole

Deep shade and the shades
Of the great surround me.
In the distance, the house
Is a ghost over grass.
You can see clear through it.

This tree is standing still,
Great names gnarling the bark
Like the names of lovers.
What were they but lovers
Of this shadowing tree?

Last evening at Kilkee
The whole sky was westward
Over the Atlantic,
No nightfall but nightfall,
Dark with the local drink.

Then, early this morning,
A small mist followed me
Halfway to this garden
Along the Galway road
And then gave way to light.

What are we but lovers,
The one web of our lives
Veined nearly visible
Over the Atlantic
As this leaf shot with light

Though its veins are darkness?
Your face is before me,
Your green eyes shot with light.
What are we as lovers
But the one leaf only?

This tree will bear others.

Listening to Fats Waller in Late Light

for Tom Molyneux, 1943–1977

Once, in a Village bar, you kept us listening
To this music till we nearly missed our train,
Then hailed a taxi half-way to the station,
Your bright tie flying behind you like a little wake.
Now we are listening into late mountain light.

A little jazz in the South of France, Vence
Maybe, or some other town in the South
Of the heart, was what you dreamed you longed for.
Wine and daylight, the company of women
And children, the slow gold raveling of an afternoon.

The year we were for Italy, you were for France,
Their local wines so distant, yet the two countries
Closer in the end than our South and your North.
You were meant to visit us in Italy,
But your lame Peugeot would never make the hills.

Back home in the coldest winter yet, you nursed
Your broad-beamed Oldsmobile like a mother
With a sick child, bundling the engine at night
With old blankets, cajoling it to hold on.
Loaded with wine, it broke down on a Maryland road.

This is America. If this were in Europe
We'd send it to you on a sunny post card,
The lake water rubbing the stones with water-lights,
The small birches lonely even in their groves.
We came from your death to this beautiful place.

The sun goes down. He's doing "Honeysuckle Rose."
Were you speaking you would no doubt tell us
There is no clean way to come to this music
Save the one long mountain road of our grief.
There is no clean way to come to this place

Save the one long mountain road dead-ending
At the landing and nothing but the sunstruck lake.
This place appeals to your love of the sunlight
As our love for you appeals to the blue
Provençal light of your early absence.

For us the North Italian, for you the Provençal,
Those two skies nearer the one color than we thought.
Now the late light shines on our luck in each other,
A wish flashed over your shoulder as you left the party.
We are cooking the small-mouth bass and listening

To Waller, drinking the white wine of Verona
Since lately we get no kick from champagne.
Lucky the woman, lucky the man, relishing
Fresh dill, a little lemon and a little butter,
A little traveling music, a particular voice

Suddenly from no place at all in particular
Wishing us to live and be happy, have fun
Somehow tapdancing barefoot on the warm floor
Going cooler as the mountain sun goes down,
And the man himself, old friend, the man is doing

"Ain't Misbehavin'." We are getting mature.

WILLIAM JAY SMITH

FROM   1998

The World below the Window

The World below the Window

The geraniums I left last night on the windowsill,
To the best of my knowledge now, are out there still,
And will be there as long as I think they will.

And will be there as long as I think that I
Can throw the window open on the sky,
A touch of geranium pink in the tail of my eye;

As long as I think I see, past leaves green-growing,
Barges moving down a river, water flowing,
Fulfillment in the thought of thought outgoing,

Fulfillment in the sight of sight replying,
Of sound in the sound of small birds southward flying,
In life life-giving, and in death undying.

Pidgin Pinch

Joe, you Big Shot! You Big Man!
You Government Issue! You Marshall Plan!

Joe, you got plenty Spearmint Gum?
I change you Money, you gimme Some!

Joe, you want Shoe-Shine, Cheap Souvenir?
My Sister overhaul you Landing Gear?

Joe, you Queer Kid? Fix-you Me?
Dig-Dig? Buzz-Buzz? Reefer? Tea?

Joe, I find you Belly Dance,
Trip Around the World—Fifty Cents!

Joe, you got Cigarette? Joe, you got Match?
Joe, you got Candy? You Sum-Bitch,

You think I Crazy? I waste my Time?
I give you *Trouble*? Gimme a *Dime*!

Now Touch the Air Softly

Now touch the air softly,
Step gently. One, two . . .
I'll love you till roses
Are robin's-egg blue;
I'll love you till gravel
Is eaten for bread,
And lemons are orange,
And lavender's red.

Now touch the air softly,
Swing gently the broom.
I'll love you till windows
Are all of a room;
And the table is laid,
And the table is bare,
And the ceiling reposes
On bottomless air.

I'll love you till Heaven
Rips the stars from his coat,
And the Moon rows away in
A glass-bottomed boat;
And Orion steps down
Like a diver below,
And Earth is ablaze
And Ocean aglow.

So touch the air softly,
And swing the broom high.
We will dust the gray mountains,
And sweep the blue sky;

And I'll love you as long
As the furrow the plow,
As However is Ever,
And Ever is Now.

Morels

A wet gray day—rain falling slowly, mist over the
   valley, mountains dark circumflex smudges in the
      distance—

Apple blossoms just gone by, the branches feathery still
   as if fluttering with half-visible antennae—

A day in May like so many in these green mountains, and
   I went out just as I had last year

At the same time, and found them there under the big
      maples—
   by the bend in the road—right where they had stood

Last year and the year before that, risen from the dark duff
   of the woods, emerging at odd angles

From spores hidden by curled and matted leaves, a fringe of
   rain on the grass around them,

Beads of rain on the mounded leaves and mosses round
   them,

Not in a ring themselves but ringed by jack-in-the-pulpits
   with deep eggplant-colored stripes;

Not ringed but rare, not gilled but polyp-like, having
   sprung up overnight—

These mushrooms of the gods, resembling human organs
   uprooted, rooted only on the air,

Looking like lungs wrenched from the human body, lungs
   reversed, not breathing internally

But being the externalization of breath itself, these
   spicy, twisted cones,

These perforated brown-white asparagus tips—these
morels,
   smelling of wet graham crackers mixed with maple
leaves;

And, reaching down by the pale green fern shoots, I
nipped
   their pulpy stems at the base

And dropped them into a paper bag—a damp brown bag
      (their
   color)—and carried

Them (weighing absolutely nothing) down the hill and
into
   the house; you held them

Under cold bubbling water and sliced them with a
surgeon's
   stroke clean through,

And sautéed them over a low flame, butter-brown; and
      we ate
   them then and there—

Tasting of the sweet damp woods and of the rain one inch
   above the meadow:

It was like feasting upon air.

Journey to the Interior

He has gone into the forest,
to the wooded mind in wrath;
he will follow out the nettles
and the bindweed path.

He is torn by tangled roots,
he is trapped by mildewed air;
he will feed on alder shoots
and on fungi: in despair

he will pursue each dry creek-bed,
each hot white gully's rough raw stone
till heaven opens overhead
a vast jawbone

and trees around grow toothpick-thin
and a deepening dustcloud swirls about
and every road leads on within
and none leads out.

The Shipwreck

Old age is a shipwreck: these thin days
we wander on a bitter alien shore
where howling wind has bent the twisted trees,
and moss-rimmed rocks rise blurred along the edge
out of a Chinese scroll.

The waves before us climb with their unending roar,
and we gather up the timbers of the ship
that broke apart:
and build, as once we did as children long ago,
lean-tos for refuge from the wind.

The fog rolls in—makes islands in the mind—
that we visit for a moment and then lose,
then find again and try again to reach
while with the swirling salt sea-spray
incessant wind moves in and carries them away.

But there are days like this when all is calm and clear:
the sun sweeps through, and we are young again,
laughing in a garden round a keg of beer,
the college towers bathed in golden light
as in a painting by Vermeer—
with the city that he saw across the river,
caught, out of time, and then recalled forever.

Galileo Galilei

Comes to knock and knock again
At a small secluded doorway
In the ordinary brain.

Into light the world is turning,
And the clocks are set for six;
And the chimney pots are smoking,
And the golden candlesticks.

Apple trees are bent and breaking,
And the heat is not the sun's;
And the Minotaur is waking,
And the streets are cattle runs.

Galileo Galilei,
In a flowing, scarlet robe,
While the stars go down the river
With the turning, turning globe,

Kneels before a black Madonna
And the angels cluster round
With grave, uplifted faces
Which reflect the shaken ground

And the orchard which is burning,
And the hills which take the light;
And the candles which have melted
On the altars of the night.

Galileo Galilei
Comes to knock and knock again
At a small secluded doorway
In the ordinary brain.

Villanelle

You rise to walk yet when you fly you sit;
The young are not so young as the old are old:
People with hair are always combing it.

The mountain now can come to Mahomet,
An offering on wings of beaten gold:
You rise to walk yet when you fly you sit.

Malherbe, whose rhetoric obscured his wit,
Read poems to his cook when dolphins bowled:
People with hair are always combing it.

This pig, the World, is roasted on a spit;
That pig today were better pigeonholed:
You rise to walk yet when you fly you sit.

We comb the country for the shoes that fit;
The mushroom grows where now the wings unfold:
People with hair are always combing it.

The laurel has been cut, the flares are lit;
The people wait, the pilot's hands are cold:
You rise to walk yet when you fly you sit;
People with hair are always combing it.

American Primitive

Look at him there in his stovepipe hat,
His high-top shoes, and his handsome collar;
Only my Daddy could look like that,
And I love my Daddy like he loves his Dollar.

The screen door bangs, and it sounds so funny—
There he is in a shower of gold;
His pockets are stuffed with folding money,
His lips are blue, and his hands feel cold.

He hangs in the hall by his black cravat,
The ladies faint, and the children holler:
Only my Daddy could look like that,
And I love my Daddy like he loves his Dollar.

The Ten

. . . one of the best-dressed ten women.

—A newspaper reference to Mme Henri Bonnet

Mme Bonnet is one of the best-dressed ten;
But what of the slovenly six, the hungry five,
The solemn three who plague all men alive,
The twittering two who appear every now and again?

What of the sexual seven who want only to please,
Advancing in unison down the hospital hall,
Conversing obscenely, wearing no clothing at all,
While under your sterile sheet you flame and freeze?

What will you say of the weird, monotonous one
Who stands beside the table when you write,
Her long hair coiling in the angry light,
Her wild eyes dancing brighter than the sun?

What will you say of her who grasps your pen
And lets the ink run slowly down your page,
Throws back her head and laughs as from a cage:
"Mme Bonnet is one, you say? . . . And then?"

Still Life

Where no one else at all was sitting,
Mabel sat,
Her fingers flying at her knitting
Like the claws of a cat.

Geraniums were planted
Like Canadian police
While dancers danced in ivory
Along the mantelpiece.

The cat on the piano took
An octave on the keys;
And wind from Tuscaloosa shook
The apple trees.

The hunched and old, anaemic moon,
Orion, and the Dog,
Wander by the cottonwood
In wisps of fog.

Red the wool upon the rug,
The curtains drawn.
Where no one else at all is going,
Mabel's gone.

Mr. Smith

How rewarding to know Mr. Smith,
   Whose writings at random appear!
Some think him a joy to be with
   While others do not, it is clear.

His eyes are somewhat Oriental,
   His fingers are notably long;
His disposition is gentle,
   He will jump at the sound of a gong.

His chin is quite smooth and uncleft,
   His face is clean-shaven and bright,
His right arm looks much like his left,
   His left leg it goes with his right.

He has friends in the arts and the sciences;
   He knows only one talent scout;
He can cope with most kitchen appliances,
   But in general prefers dining out.

When young he collected matchboxes,
   He now collects notebooks and hats;
He has eaten *roussettes* (flying foxes),
   Which are really the next thing to bats!

He has never set foot on Majorca,
   He has been to Tahiti twice,
But will seldom, no veteran walker,
   Take two steps when one will suffice.

He abhors motorbikes and boiled cabbage;
   Zippers he just tolerates;

He is wholly indifferent to cribbage,
  And cuts a poor figure on skates.

He weeps by the side of the ocean,
  And goes back the way that he came;
He calls out his name with emotion—
  It returns to him always the same.

It returns on the wind and he hears it
  While the waves make a rustle around;
The dark settles down, and he fears it,
  He fears its thin, crickety sound.

He thinks more and more as time passes,
  Rarely opens a volume on myth.
Until mourned by the tall prairie grasses,
  How rewarding to know Mr. Smith!

BARRY SPACKS

FROM   1982
Spacks Street

Blind in His Sorrow

Blind in his sorrow and his fitful joy
he travels through the tangled wood of self
while she moves on beside him, meadow-sweet.

He blunders in the dark, afraid to see
how always she, beside him and before
makes everywhere a clearing; everywhere.

He stands upon his shadow's shrunken noon,
and if he'd take one step he'd come into
her love, that waits for him, a summer field.

Three Songs for My Daughter

I
Simply as the world is turning
Toward the ashes and the fuel,
Toward the secret of the burning
Simply as the world is turning
Children cross the road to school.

Many come to less by growing
Once the autumn's courses start.
Daughter, in the place you're going
Many come to less by growing,
Losing what they've had by heart.

Simply as the world is turning,
Scholar hand in hand with fool,
To a learning and unlearning
Simply as the world is turning
Children cross the road to school.

2
Child, where we stand
Is quicksand.

This venerable crust
Dust.

Move bravely on,
As if there were watchers.

3
Daughter, you will reach a twilight

Clear as joy: a summer evening
When the small bells ring and fingers
Stir within too swift for meaning.
Take the hand of your beloved;
In the bell of stillness gathered
Time will seem to pause for you.
Dear passenger: just so, so still
With us, until the rhyme for darkness
Booms—booms as if the feathers
Of all scattered birds were falling.
Night comes. Our voices, pounding,
Are the bells
That will your love.

My Clothes

Poor spineless things, the clothes I've shed
in hopes of the essential bed
of love. Like chastened dogs they wait
to be forgiven, stroked, pulled straight.
I lift them to the light, all holes
and patches, all the outworn roles,
the Dandy's musty ornaments,
the Lover's, and the Malcontent's.
The day seeks like a wind its form;
my clothes have kept me from the storm.
From age to age though I emerge
from cloying silks or common serge
my mere limbs stutter in the sun;
outside the cave, I come undone.
O, voices in your nakedness,
great dreamers in your skins or less,
make golden ages fill my mind
where ease leaves agony behind
and passion, all her raiment gone,
is beautiful with nothing on.

Recommendations

This is a good fellow
   who knows what he may do?
He is most excited, he is walking
   the walls of himself
on tiptoe. Give him
   a prize.

And this one is steady;
   it is clear that he is breathing;
he will never kill any number
   of old ladies, nor harrow
hell. Give him
   a prize.

Glory Learnt from Roses

One time she gave me roses,
Such purely overcome
Infatuated roses, fierce
But delicate their bloom,

That I who'd balked at yielding
To keep my spirit free
Aspired to strive like roses—
To live less meagerly.

I'd understood her roses:
Extravagance they meant—
And grew myself full-hearted
Studying their scent.

As petals fell I studied
To make autumnal sense;
Observed that slowest raining:
A thousand weigh an ounce.

She'd sent a gift of roses
And roses told me all:
How past their will they open,
How past their will they fall.

That's glory learnt from roses,
Whatever weight of hurt
Is bound to follow after
The blooming of the heart.

Neilsen

"They called me Battling Nelson," said Neilsen,
my neighbor. "Assumed I was Irish . . . fought
my way to school and back, plus home
for lunch—there's something I can't understand!"
(Somebody's parking a car at his curb)—
"What do they think, they live in my house?"
Or he's up on the roof, age 76,
brooming away the snow. "Insane,"
my daughter says, "it insulates."
We shrug, we both say: "Neilsen"—Neilsen's
throwing a stone at a dog, it's not
his dog, why use his tree?—each fall
he clears the leaves to his very boundary,
exact. I guess that all along
with his passion for neatness and property
he'd wanted only this: "O world,
MAKE SENSE!" "You boys! Get off that wall!
Is that your wall? is that your wall?"

TIMOTHY STEELE

FROM   1994
The Color Wheel

Aurora

Your sleep is so profound
This room seems a recess
Awaiting consciousness.
Gauze curtains, drawn around
The postered bed, confute
Each waking attribute—
Volition, movement, sound.

Outside, though, chilly light
Shivers a puddle's coil
Of iridescent oil;
Windows, sun-struck, ignite;
Doves strut along the edge
Of roof- and terrace-ledge
And drop off into flight.

And soon enough you'll rise.
Long-gowned and self-aware,
Brushing life through your hair,
You'll notice with surprise
The way your glass displays,
Twin-miniatured, your face
In your reflective eyes.

Goddess, it's you in whom
Our clear hearts joy and chafe.
Awaken, then. Vouchsafe
Ideas to resume.
Draw back the drapes: let this
Quick muffled emphasis
Flood light across the room.

Beatitudes, While Setting Out
the Trash

The sparrow in the fig tree cocks his head
And tilts at, so to speak, his daily bread
(The sunset's stunningly suffused with gold).
A squirrel on the lawn rears and inspects
A berry in its paws and seems to hold
The pose of a Tyrannosaurus Rex.

The clothesline's plaids and stripes perform some snaps;
A page of blown newspaper smartly wraps
A fire hydrant in the day's events;
And there's engaging, if pedestrian, song
Ringing its changes from a chain-link fence
A boy with a backpack walks a stick along.

I park my rattling dolly at the curb
And set the trash among leaves gusts disturb.
Then, hands tucked in my sweatshirt's pocket-muff,
A mammal cousin of the kangaroo,
I watch my breath contrive a lucent puff
Out of lung-exhalated CO_2.

Small breath, small warmth, but what is that to me?
My steps re-traced, the bird's still in his tree:
He grooms, by nuzzling, a raised underwing;
He shakes and sends a shiver through his breast,
As if, from where he perches, counseling
That *Blessed are the meek*, for they are blest.

Portrait of the Artist as a Young Child

Your favorite crayon is Midnight Blue
(Hurrah for dark dramatic skies!)
Though inwardly it makes you groan
To see it like an ice-cream cone
Shrink with too zealous exercise.

But soon you're offering for review
Sheets where Magenta flowers blaze.
And here's a field whose mass and weight
Incontrovertibly indicate
You're in your Burnt Sienna phase.

Long may you study color, pore
Over Maroon, Peach, Pine Green, Teal.
I think of my astonishment
When I first saw the spectrum bent
Around into a color wheel,

A disc of white there at the core,
The outer colors vivid, wild.
Red, with its long wavelengths, met
With much-refracted violet,
And all with all were reconciled.

When I look past you now, I see
The winter amaryllis bloom
Above its terra-cotta pot
Whose earthen orange-apricot
Lends warmth to the entire room.

And cherry and mahogany
Introduce tones of brown and plum;
While by the hearth a basket holds
Balls of yarn—purples, greens, and golds
That you may wear in years to come.

Yet for the moment you dispense
Color again. Again you kneel:
Your left hand spread out, holding still
The paper you'll with fervor fill,
You're off and traveling through the wheel

Of contrasts and of complements,
Where every shade divides and blends,
Where you find those that you prefer,
Where being is not linear,
But bright and deep, and never ends.

Pacific Rim

Unsteadily, I stand against the wash
Flooding in, climbing thigh, waist, rib-cage. Turning,
It sweeps me, breaststroking, out on its swift
Sudsy withdrawal. Greenly, a wave looms;
I duck beneath its thundering collapse,
Emerging on the far side, swimming hard
For the more manageable, deeper waters.
How the sea elevates! Pausing to tread it
And feather-kicking its profundity,
The swimmer wears each swell around his neck,
And rides the slopes that heave through him,
The running valleys that he sinks across,
Part of the comprehensive element
Washing as well now the Galápagos,
The bay at Wenchow, the Great Barrier Reef.

Why, then, this ache, this sadness? Toweled off,
The flesh is mortified, the small hairs standing
Among their goose bumps, the teeth chattering
Within the skull. A brutal century
Draws to a close. Bewildering genetrix,
As your miraculous experiment
In consciousness hangs in the balance, do
You pity those enacting it? The headlands'
Blunt contours sloping to the oceanside,
Do angels weep for our folly? Merciful,
Do you accompany our mortality
Just as, low to the water, the pelican
Swiftly pursues his shadow down a swell?

DAVID ST. JOHN

FROM   1985
Hush

Elegy

They've carried the fat man who yelled
For more butter on his lobster through the streets
Weeping. No, not the man the people are weeping & a
   whole city
Is domed with auroras & smoke. The fat man's dead.
Only the sea is silent about it, everyone else
Is carrying on, & the pucker of lye & revolt washed the
   rough
Mouth of the harbor. That man walked his mornings
By the shore. He dragged a brazen,
Wooden woman in off the beach, & nailed her
To the thick beam of the ceiling, where she looked out
For bad weather & Chile. Hung the wall with a ship's
Wheel, so that the moon lit the brass & copper spokes
            & such an odd star
Led him back, always, to this room overlooking the waves.
The sign of the crab shifts across the horizon. The sorrow
Of night. He is laid out like an old sea lion,
Not so much exhausted as worn: Of taking
That chance of saying what pleases you, such as the truth.
Or some few words that sound like music & the sea.
That please you. That come & go.
As easily as government of tides, or the vandals & soldiers
Sacking your house. As the blossoms of lilac draping the
   casket.
Of all simple things, the simplest: Your lashes
Locked together. A little earth.

Hush

for my son

The way a tired Chippewa woman
Who's lost a child gathers up black feathers,
Black quills & leaves
That she wraps & swaddles in a little bale, a shag
Cocoon she carries with her & speaks to always
As if it were the child,
Until she knows the soul has grown fat & clever,
That the child can find its own way at last;
Well, I go everywhere
Picking the dust out of the dust, scraping the breezes
Up off the floor, & gather them into a doll
Of you, to touch at the nape of the neck, to slip
Under my shirt like a rag—the way
Another man's wallet rides above his heart. As you
Cry out, as if calling to a father you conjure
In the paling light, the voice rises, instead, in me.
Nothing stops it, the crying. Not the clove of moon,
Not the woman raking my back with her words. Our letters
Close. Sometimes, you ask
About the world; sometimes, I answer back. Nights
Return you to me for a while, as sleep returns sleep
To a landscape ravaged
& familiar. The dark watermark of your absence, a hush.

ADRIEN STOUTENBURG

FROM   1986

Land of Superior Mirages

Mote

The hummingbird, acquaintance,
hanging at the feeder,
fencing with his beak,
suspended as by whirling arms
or two round harps,
is instant color.

Here we have a minute thunder,
mandolin, banjo, fever,
potential crisis of motion
as in a spinning jenny
grown eccentric, its cotton raveling
into a knot like a flower.

This spinner ends in rainbow,
and so begins.
(The inside of the egg, surely,
is a centrifuge of opals.)

He rests, rarely and neatly,
after his spike explores
honey trapped in glass and jasmine.
He goes to that rest so swiftly
he is nearly a myth. He becomes
a bud on a twig of a bough.
He dives into wind as into water.
He lifts himself, or is lifted,
into a feathered diamond
greener than the leaves
he brings his light to.

He is an uncertain visitor,
unpredictable, fickle, late to appointments,
obsessed with nectar in distant cabinets.

But when he comes, shining the window,
and leans there, gleams in his cape,
tips his javelin and remains,
we lay down our books, music, cards,
and watch like the cats
who are also our boarders,
as helpless as they
to stay that mote by talons or love.

Tree Service

Jockey, juggler, rider of ropes and leaves,
climber with metal thorns nailed to his feet,
he kicks dust back, stomps upward on his spurs
until his yellow bump hat bobs and gleams
among the antlers of a dying beast.

I could not save it, and it hung too near
with blackening horns aimed for the house,
but I am bothered by this hired shape
going up through the dead lace of boughs
that never felt a sharper tooth than sleet.

Yet I must back him since his life is pitched
against an overgrown and staglike head
assembling ruin above my roof,
though dreading the first severed branch
and its steep plunge.
                          It falls, scattering rot
like chaff from a broken star; more sky moves in
but I miss the reaching claw. A hoof goes next—
it paced for years above my fires and mist—
and I perceive how easily space grows
around a saw.
                          He swings and sears,
agile as a toy, the round hat floating
like a crown. I feel an office worker's awe
for his hard bustling thighs and arms.

Only the rough, round trunk remains.
A portion falls, the sound heart glowing red
against a litter of gray, scattered veins,

witness to how communication failed
between the blowing top and the dark nerves
that worked in ignorance to feed a dying crest.

The saw is still at last, and still the great stump
throbs and shines, the hidden taproot busy as before,
cell, core, and tissue storing useless fat.
The sky looks bare. The wind is high and keen;
it draws a knife against my back.

Message

Something has caught in my throat,
neither frog nor bone,
more like a fork
that tastes of alum,
or a stone that has lived in fire,
possibly a jewel
(the ruby's red glass furnace),
perhaps a diamond, unpolished
(white eye in darkness),
or simply my own breath
grown jagged,
trapped between speech and silence.

There is no surgeon for this,
or not one near enough
this high-pitched place
whirled round by mountains
and the wind's unfettered voice.

I shall learn sign language
but even then the stone
or fork or fire, desire's impediment,
will make my hands stutter.

Consider this when next I call
or try to signal
across mesas, thunder, gulfs,
and the garrulous crosses
of telephone poles.

Evening might be the best time,
when I am a silhouette—
or some deep morning
when, in stillness, you could catch the beat—
the clear and strenuous tone—
of that fixed voice
where my heart swings
in its round perch,
alone, yet not alone.

Self-Portrait

In this sketch I am in a canoe
as silver as a young moon,
and the water is so still
it hums with the pickerel's delicate teeth.
The water is so deep
the sunfish's lantern burns out,
and my hook is a steel question mark
hanging upsidedown in all the night
the lake hauls to itself
from forests, scum, or passing rot.

I am wearing a white shirt,
the sleeves pushed up,
and at my feet a jug of wine rolls
like a round, glass child.
My tackle box is trim,
and a painted bobber winks
above the barb designed
to lure some hunger underneath.

It is all deceit—
the boat, the gaff hook, net, and knife,
props only for a chance to watch, alone,
the light and wind and perchless sky.
I dread the least tug at the line,
the gasping weight, the wounded throat,
but the risk of blood, as everywhere, is great.

Drumcliffe: Passing By

Cast a cold Eye
On Life, on Death.
Horseman, pass by!

W. B. YEATS'S TOMBSTONE

It was rain and green and always rain,
and the May cold spilling through rock walls
into bone-walls and brain, caught in the folds
of clothing and breath, dripping where farmers walked
like swimmers trapped in weedy boots,
hissing on hedges and dogs and death.
Rain has its home there, building ditches, ruins,
and green-haired wives.
                At Yeats's grave,
under a black umbrella's roof,
I understand how rarely blue exists
and how, no doubt, his poet's skull
lies packed with moss in less than thirty years
beneath his plain, admonishing stone.

The rooks were noisy rags in blowing trees.
Swallows, as neat as bats, dived through mist
for their winged food.
              No horseman I,
but still a rider through rain and green
and dusk, casting a cold eye.

Contributors

JOHN BRICUTH is the poetic alter ego of John T. Irwin, Decker
Professor in the Humanities at the Johns Hopkins
University and former chair for almost twenty years of the
Writing Seminars. A former editor of *The Georgia Review*,
Irwin now edits the fiction and poetry series at the Johns
Hopkins University Press. His most recent volume of criti-
cism, *The Mystery to a Solution*, won the Christian Gauss
Prize from Phi Beta Kappa for the best scholarly book in
the humanities in 1994 and the Scaglione Prize from the
Modern Language Association for the best scholarly book
in comparative literature. John Bricuth's volumes of
poetry are *The Heisenberg Variations* and *Just Let Me Say
This about That*.

JOHN BURT teaches English and American literature at Brandeis
University. He is the author of two books of poems,
They Way Down (1988) and *Work without Hope* (1996). He
is completing a new book of poems, to be called *Victory*.
All three of his books have a strong investment in narrative
poetry in blank verse, frequently on historical subjects. In
addition to his poetic work, he is the editor of *The Collected
Poems of Robert Penn Warren* (1998). He is also writing a
historical and philosophical study of the Lincoln-Douglas
debates of 1858.

THOMAS CARPER is the author of three collections of metrical
verse: *Fiddle Lane*, *From Nature*, and *Distant Blue*, the recipi-
ent of the 2003 Richard Wilbur Award. With the British
scholar Derek Attridge, he is coauthor of *Meter and Mean-
ing: An Introduction to Rhythm in Poetry*. He has taught at
the University of Southern Maine, and with his wife, Janet,

he sings in the Cornish Trio, performing a cappella Rennaissance motets and madrigals.

PHILIP DACEY's poems have appeared in *Poetry*, *Esquire*, *The Nation*, *American Review*, *Paris Review*, and *Partisan Review*. Dacey's eighth full-length collection is *The Mystery of Max Schmitt: Poems on the Life and Work of Thomas Eakins* (2004). His awards include two fellowships from the National Endowment for the Arts, a New York YM-YWHA Discovery Award, and three Pushcart Prizes. He recently completed a book of sonnets and a book of poems about Walt Whitman. He teaches at Southwest State University in Minnesota.

TOM DISCH is the author of nine books of poetry, thirteen novels, five story collections, three critical books, and "enough paintings to cover a football field." His latest book is *The Castle of Perseverance: Job Opportunities in Contemporary Poetry* (2001). He is an art reviewer for both *The Weekly Standard* and *The New York Sun* and has been awarded the Michael Braude Award from the American Academy of Arts and Letters.

EMILY GROSHOLZ is a professor of philosophy at the Pennsylvania State University and the author of four books of poetry. She has been an advisory editor for *The Hudson Review* for twenty years. The author of books on Descartes, Leibniz, and the philosophy of mathematics, she has also edited collections of essays on Maxine Kumin, W. E. B. Du Bois, and Simone de Beauvoir. She lives with her husband, the medievalist Robert R. Edwards, and their four children in State College, Pennsylvania.

VICKI HEARNE published three volumes of poetry: *Nervous Horses*, *In the Absence of Horses*, and *The Parts of Light*. She was also the author of *Adam's Task: Calling Animals by Name*, *Bandit: Dossier of a Dangerous Dog*, and *Animal Happiness*. A writer and animal trainer, Hearne was a visiting fellow at Yale University's Institution for Social and Policy Studies and a contributing editor of *Harper's*. She was a recipient of the Ingram Merrill Distinguished Achievement Award and the Academy of American Poets' Peter I. B. Lavan Award. She died in 2001.

JOHN HOLLANDER has published eighteen books of poetry and six volumes of criticism and edited many anthologies and collections; his most recent books are *Picture Window* and a collection of twentieth-century American comic verse, *American Wits*. Among other awards, he has received the Bollingen Prize, the Levinson Prize, and a MacArthur Fellowship, and he is currently Sterling Professor Emeritus of English at Yale.

JOSEPHINE JACOBSEN was the author of seven books of poetry, two works of criticism, and three collections of short fiction. From 1971 to 1973 she served two terms as Consultant in Poetry to the Library of Congress, a post now called Poet Laureate. Her many awards included a 1994 Academy of Arts citation, the Lenore Marshall Poetry Prize, a fellowship from the Academy of American Poets for service to poetry, and the selection of *On the Island: Short Stories* as one of the five nominees for the PEN/Faulkner fiction award. Other honors include an award from the American Academy of Arts and Letters and eight inclusions of her stories in the *O. Henry Prize Stories*. Her volume *In the*

Crevice of Time was a finalist for the National Book Award
in poetry in 1995. She died in 2003.

X. J. KENNEDY taught English at the University of Michigan, the
Woman's College of the University of North Carolina
(now UNC–Greensboro), and Tufts University before
leaving to write full time in 1978. He has published six col-
lections of poetry, including *Nude Descending a Staircase*,
which won the 1961 Academy of American Poets' Lamont
Prize; *Cross Ties*, awarded the 1985 *Los Angeles Times* Book
Prize; and *The Lords of Misrule, Poems 1992–2001* (2002),
which received the Poet's Prize. He has also written eight-
een children's books, including *Exploding Gravy* (2002), and
has coauthored several textbooks, including, with Dana
Gioia, *An Introduction to Poetry*, now in its tenth edition.
His numerous honors include the Aiken Taylor Award
for Lifetime Achievement in Modern American Poetry,
Guggenheim and National Arts Council fellowships, the
Shelley Memorial Award, the Golden Rose of the New
England Poetry Club, the Michael Braude Award for Light
Verse, and the National Council of Teachers of English
Award for Excellence in Poetry for Children. He lives with
his wife, Dorothy, in Lexington, Massachusetts.

CHARLES MARTIN's new verse translation of the *Metamorphoses* of
Ovid was published in 2004, and his fourth book of poems,
Starting from Sleep: New and Selected Poems, was published
in 2002. Other books include *Steal the Bacon* and *What the
Darkness Proposes*, both nominated for the Pulitzer Prize; a
translation of the poems of Catullus; and a critical intro-
duction to the Latin poet's work. He is the recipient of a
Bess Hokin Award from *Poetry*, a 2001 Pushcart Prize, and
fellowships from the Ingram Merrill Foundation and the

National Endowment for the Arts. A professor at Queensborough Community College (CUNY), he has recently taught workshops at the Sewanee Writers' Conference, the West Chester Conference on Form and Narrative in Poetry, and the Unterberg Center of the Ninety-Second Street YMHA.

ROBERT PACK has published eighteen books of poetry, most recently, *Elk in Winter* (2004), *Rounding It Out* (1999), *Minding the Sun* (1996), and *Fathering the Map: New and Selected Later Poems* (1993). His most recent book of criticism, *Belief and Uncertainty in the Poetry of Robert Frost*, was published in 1993. He is currently completing a book about Shakespeare's major plays, *Choice and Necessity*, and teaching at the Honors College of the University of Montana.

ROBERT PHILLIPS is poetry editor of the *Texas Review* and a councilor of the Texas Institute of Letters. He teaches at the University of Houston, where he was director of the Creative Writing Program. Phillips recently published a collection of his short stories, *News about People You Know*, and his seventh collection of poems will appear in 2005. His edition of *Creative Glut: Selected Essays by Karl Shapiro* will be published in 2004.

WYATT PRUNTY is Carlton Professor of English at the University of the South and the author of seven collections of poetry, his most recent being *Unarmed and Dangerous: New and Selected Poems*. A critical work on contemporary poetry, *"Fallen from the Symboled World": Precedents for the New Formalism*, was published in 1990 and an edited collection of essays, *Sewanee Writers on Writing*, was published in 2000. The recipient of a grant from the Rockefeller Foundation, a Guggenheim Fellowship, a Johns Hopkins Fellowship, and a Brown Foundation Fellowship, he is the director of the Sewanee Writers' Conference and general editor of the Sewanee Writers' Series.

GIBBONS RUARK's poems have appeared widely for nearly forty years in such magazines as *Ploughshares, The New Republic, The New Yorker,* and *Poetry* and in various anthologies and texts. They have also won awards that include three Poetry Fellowships from the National Endowment for the Arts and a Pushcart Prize. Previously collected in *A Program for Survival, Reeds, Keeping Company, Small Rain, Forms of Retrieval,* and *Rescue the Perishing,* seventy of his poems appear in *Passing through Customs: New and Selected Poems,* published in 1999. Ruark has taught English at the University of Delaware since 1968.

WILLIAM JAY SMITH, the author of more than fifty books of poetry, children's verse, literary criticism, translation, and memoirs, and the editor of several influential anthologies, served as Consultant in Poetry to the Library of Congress, a position now called Poet Laureate, from 1968 to 1970. His translations have won awards from the French Academy, the Swedish Academy, and the Hungarian government. Two of his thirteen collections of poetry were final contenders for the National Book Award. Professor Emeritus of English at Hollins University and a member of the American Academy of Arts and Letters, he divides his time between Cummington, Massachusetts, and Paris.

BARRY SPACKS has published about 450 poems in journals, two novels, and nine poetry collections. His *Spacks Street: New and Selected Poems* won the Commonwealth Club of California's Poetry Medal. He has also put in many years of teaching at the Massachusetts Institute of Technology and the University of California, Santa Barbara. His compact disc, *A Private Reading*, contains a selection of forty-two poems (plus chat) from fifty years of work.

TIMOTHY STEELE has published three collections of poems, *Uncertainties and Rest* (1979), *Sapphics against Anger and Other Poems* (1986), and *The Color Wheel* (1994), and a volume of literary criticism, *Missing Measures: Modern Poetry and the Revolt against Meter* (1990). More recently, he has edited *The Poems of J. V. Cunningham* (1997) and published *All the Fun's in How You Say a Thing: an Explanation of Meter and Versification* (1999). Steele's honors include a Guggenheim Fellowship, a Peter I. B. Lavan Younger Poets Award from the Academy of American Poets, the Los Angeles PEN Center's Literary Award for Poetry, and the Robert Fitzgerald Award for the study of prosody. Born in 1948 in Burlington, Vermont, Steele has lived in Los Angeles since 1977. Currently, he is a professor of English at California State University, Los Angeles.

DAVID ST. JOHN's most recent collections are *Study for the World's Body* (1994), which was nominated for the National Book Award in Poetry, *The Red Leaves of Night* (1999), *Prism* (2002), and *The Face: A Novella in Verse* (2004). Among his numerous awards are the Rome Fellowship in Literature and an award in literature from the American Academy of Arts and Letters, and the O. B. Hardison, Jr., Prize, a career award for teaching and writing, from the Folger Shakespeare Library. He is the director of the Program in Literature and Creative Writing at the University of Southern California.

ADRIEN STOUTENBURG wrote more than forty books before her
death in 1982. Many, written under the pseudonym of Lace
Kendall, were for children. She received the Academy of
American Poets' Lamont Poetry Award and two citations
from the Poetry Society of America.

POETRY TITLES IN THE SERIES

John Hollander, *"Blue Wine" and Other Poems*
Robert Pack, *Waking to My Name: New and Selected Poems*
Philip Dacey, *The Boy under the Bed*
Wyatt Prunty, *The Times Between*
Barry Spacks, *Spacks Street: New and Selected Poems*
Gibbons Ruark, *Keeping Company*
David St. John, *Hush*
Wyatt Prunty, *What Women Know, What Men Believe*
Adrien Stoutenberg, *Land of Superior Mirages: New and Selected Poems*
John Hollander, *In Time and Place*
Charles Martin, *Steal the Bacon*
John Bricuth, *The Heisenberg Variations*
Tom Disch, *Yes, Let's: New and Selected Poems*
Wyatt Prunty, *Balance as Belief*
Tom Disch, *Dark Verses and Light*
Thomas Carper, *Fiddle Lane*
Emily Grosholz, *Eden*
X. J. Kennedy, *Dark Horses*
Wyatt Prunty, *The Run of the House*
Robert Phillips, *Breakdown Lane*
Vicki Hearne, *The Parts of Light*
Timothy Steele, *The Color Wheel*
Josephine Jacobsen, *In the Crevice of Time: New and Collected Poems*
Thomas Carper, *From Nature*
John Burt, *Work without Hope*
Charles Martin, *What the Darkness Proposes*
Wyatt Prunty, *Since the Noon Mail Stopped*
William Jay Smith, *The World below the Window: Poems, 1937–1997*
Wyatt Prunty, *Unarmed and Dangerous: New and Selected Poems*
Robert Phillips, *Spinach Days*
John T. Irwin, ed. *Words Brushed by Music: Twenty-Five Years of the Johns Hopkins Poetry Series*

Credits